Head's Tales

Sandra Gordon

Head's Tales

Copyright © 2007 Sandra Gordon

The moral right of the author has been asserted.

Apart from any fair dealing for the purposes of research or private study, or criticism or review, as permitted under the Copyright, Designs and Patents Act 1988, this publication may only be reproduced, stored or transmitted, in any form or by any means, with the prior permission in writing of the publishers, or in the case of reprographic reproduction in accordance with the terms of licences issued by the Copyright Licensing Agency. Enquiries concerning reproduction outside those terms should be sent to the publishers.

Matador
9 De Montfort Mews
Leicester LE1 7FW, UK
Tel: (+44) 116 255 9311 / 9312
Email: books@troubador.co.uk
Web: www.troubador.co.uk/matador

ISBN: 978-1905886-630

Typeset in 12pt Bembo by Troubador Publishing Ltd, Leicester, UK

Matador is an imprint of Troubador Publishing Ltd

Printed and bound by Cromwell Press, Trowbridge, Wiltshire

Dedicated to my husband and family who light up my life, to my golden friends who support me strongly and to the hundreds of children, teachers and colleagues it has been my good fortune to know.

Contents

Chapter 1	The Early Years	1
Chapter 2	Stepping Out	24
Chapter 3	It's for real, folks.	31
Chapter 4	Down South	52
Chapter 5	Reality check ahead	65
Chapter 6	Life changes	82
Chapter 7	Who am I?	89
Chapter 8	Land of the Celts	100
Chapter 9	A new beginning	112
Chapter 10	Flash Gordon	137
Chapter 11	Taking Stock and moving on	148
Chapter 12	Choosing our motor-home.	164
Chapter 13	The big six-oh!	192
Chapter 14	The living's not easy	201
Chapter 15	At last – grandchildren	209
Chapter 16	Tips for 1st time travellers	218
Chapter 17	Full Circle	223

CHAPTER 1

The Early Years

I am an only child. I was born in Newcastle-upon-Tyne during austere times, just as the war ended. No fat children then, I can assure you. I was lucky because my parents were both only children or so they thought, but more of that later. As a consequence I had two doting sets of grandparents so I wanted for nothing and I had no brothers or sisters to share with. For the first six years of my life I lived with my parents and grandparents in a large apartment on the western outskirts of Newcastle. My mother had been given a dowry on marrying but she and my father spent the lot on holidays and luxuries instead of a house. Consequently, when I was seven we ended up in a council house. My father was a staunch socialist and said he could not own a house because it was immoral. This was an excuse of course. It took him twenty years to change his mind and give in to my mother's wish to buy a home.

Newcastle was a lovely city. I have vivid memories of taking the clanking yellow trolley bus, that produced bright sparks from the overhead trolleys as it sped along, into the town and spending time in the shops and the parks that surrounded the town. We always returned home before tea-time as in those days drunken men lolled around the pavements when the pubs closed, and I was not allowed to see such things. My grandfather and I often went on the bus to the terminus, Denton Square, at the edge of the city to walk in the fields and feed the chickens and ducks.

My schooling was pretty ordinary. I attended a number of small primaries then a county grammar school. These were happy years with very few worries.

As I grew up I joined the youth group at John Knox Presbyterian Church in West Denton, as many did in those days. It was one of the only places for young people to gather. Here I met a lot of good folk, many of whom became life-long friends. I also met my husband, Henry, to whom, after 39 years, I am still married, (loud fanfare of trumpets, however after he reads this book that situation could change.) We have travelled many paths together, he becoming a clergyman and me a teacher.

Over the years we have moved around the country. My husband was very happy as a clergyman, firstly in the Presbyterian Church of England and then in the United Reformed Church, and I climbed the rungs of the educational ladder. I then decided to take a new path and began to lead school inspections. In other words as my niece, an English teacher, tells me I have joined forces with 'the dark side.' She does not own up to having an aunt who leads inspections.

Throughout my travels I have learnt that success and happiness are not always measured in what we do or what we have, but more in what we are, how we grow and develop as individuals and in what we receive from others. I have been very lucky to have had the luxury of being able to buy what I wanted as well as what I needed and yes, I have had the joy of reaching the top of my career. However, I have also experienced what poverty means, seen just as much sorrow and at times been just as sad as the next person. On many occasions I have trusted the wrong people and paid the price. I have made the wrong decisions and had to perform a discreet about turn. I reckon many of us have, but perhaps are too naïve or embarrassed to share the experience or to believe others could be suffering the same. Throughout my wanderings happiness has appeared and disappeared many times. It is an elusive commodity and has no hooks upon which to hang securely.

On reading about my journey through life I hope others will laugh and despair with me but more than that, I hope it will help them to understand their own journey. By the end of the tale, I hope it will confirm that we alone are responsible for our life, but we are not alone in the experiences that may confront us. Others have been there and survived. I wonder now if, given a second chance, I would change anything on my journey– well if you read until the end you may find out.

My story contains no high-powered language as I cannot stand jargon, especially educational jargon. If a teacher, of all people, cannot talk plainly and simply then there is not much hope for the rest of the population. Of course I excuse science teachers from this comment, as they do have a habit of speaking in a language all their own. In no way do I assume that my ideas are correct or that I am a fount of all knowledge and have found the answers to everything. I simply know my discoveries and findings have served me well over a successful career and helped me to remain reasonably stable and happily married for nearly forty years.

I was a happy child, though very 'delicate.' Before I was six months old I had measles. Vaccinations for these illnesses did not exist in the 1940's. On a chance encounter whilst shopping a child leaned over my pram and coughed all over me, spreading the dreaded measles infection, before my mother could stop her. Consequently I was extremely ill and required careful nursing for many weeks and lost vision in one eye. My mother took me to the eye hospital every week for five years for innovative treatment to restore the muscle and some vision.

My earliest memories of treatment for my eye are of sitting on a high stool in a room at St. Mary's Eye Hospital in Newcastle with a patch over one eye and the other pressed to a large contraption of a machine, trying to either place a lion in a cage or a little girl on a swing. The pungent smell of the iodine and the bright yellow patches held over eyes by the many children sitting in the queue waiting for treatment stayed with me all through my life. Wherever I smell this now I am immediately transported back to that eye-hospital. The treatment worked, but I am sure this hassle is what stopped my mother having any more children. Or it could have been that I was a horrible little brat, but I don't think so.

I cannot remember a time when I did not wear glasses. At first they were the round, owl-like, tortoise shell trimmed National Health Service glasses held on by ribbon, as my habit was to throw my head back when laughing and the glasses flew off. My hair was long so the ribbon could be hidden beneath and no one noticed. Naturally I had to get used to used to all the usual ' four eyes' jokes as soon as I began school. Also, having sight in only one eye made me extra cautious of new things and of tackling new situations. I have never really overcome this reticence.

Before I was six, I spent a lot of time at home ill with tonsillitis. My mother taught me to read and count and I never fell behind at school. My grandfather taught me to do neat, copperplate handwriting that won me prizes in national handwriting competitions. When I was at home ill, I would watch him carefully as he gingerly repaired the smallest watches. He was a meticulous clockmaker, a courteous and well-mannered gentleman and his patience and determination to succeed, to a certain extent, rubbed off on me.

Every summer weekend my mother and I were taken to the County Cricket match, as my father was an avid supporter. To this day I think my mother only went because if she had not my father would have gone without her. He was very much a male of his age. He was kind and caring but boss in the house. The picnic basket was filled with goodies and I took a bat and ball to play with on the adjacent field. I have disliked picnics and cricket to this day. One hot and sunny Saturday afternoon I felt really ill with a raging sore throat and collapsed. I had septicaemia caused by poisoned tonsils. I was taken to hospital and the offending tonsils were removed.

There were no caring children's wards then. The 'all-seeing' sister regularly patrolled pristine wards that reeked of disinfectant. She ruled over fiercesome and cleanly starched nurses whose aprons crackled loudly as they moved. Germs would not dare exist in the midst of such extreme cleanliness. It is a shame wards today do not meet the same high standards.

After I was admitted my mother was asked to leave. She waved me goodbye and promised to come back in the evening. I was astonished that I was expected to undo and remove my liberty bodice without any help. If you have ever worn such a ridiculous thing as a liberty bodice with hundreds of little buttons down the front, you will know exactly what I mean. If you haven't, then don't even go there. Some nurses were lovely but the occasional one was awful. I remember the day of the operation vividly. All the children sat on the end bed waiting for their turn. My surname began with 'W', so I was last.

I saw lively, chatty children being wheeled away and quiet and sleeping children returning. When I was wheeled into the theatre I was surrounded by white tiled walls, bright lights and lots of people in green and white. A masked man asked me to be a 'clever girl' and blow up the balloon for him. The balloon was black, ugly and smelled disgustingly of rubber. I recall the smell to this day. I was, of course, a good girl and tried to blow it up as instructed. On awaking I was sick in my bed and reprimanded by the nurse for creating extra work. I was given crisps to eat by a masochistic nurse and jelly to eat by a sensitive and sweet nurse. I recovered but have hated hospitals to this day. The best part of this whole process was coming home, finding a new doll on the table for me and special ice-cream for tea.

I loved school for it is lonely as an only child with no one at home to talk to, play or fight with. I had friends home regularly but it is not the same. Some friends offered to sell me one of their brothers or sisters! I read avidly and this took me into other realms. My daughter has the same habit. We can still begin a book in the morning and be oblivious to all around, continuing to read until evening if we are enjoying it. School ploughed on as school does. I loved playing schools at home and was always the bossy teacher. This was perhaps a first inkling of what I would spend my lifetime doing – playing at schools from the other side of the desk.

I remember my first day at school, seeing a sandpit for the first time and not wanting to play with anything else. I was very shy and too scared to ask to go to the toilet so the inevitable happened. I had to stand in the corner in disgrace and was so mortified I never did it again. I have, throughout my career, let children go to the toilet whenever they ask. I was always small for my age and given parts such as 'Thumbelina' in the school pantomime at Christmas. How I longed for a few more inches so I could play the giant but it was just not to be. All my life I have longed to 'see' when in a crowd and to be able to reach things from the top shelf in the cupboard or the supermarket. I have longed to kiss my husband without standing on my toes. Only later in life did we finally find out why I was quite small. So, if a small person asks you to reach something for them in the supermarket do be kind to them and sympathise please.

Mind you, I was certainly not a 'goody two shoes' at school. Many days I would hide my stinging hands from my parents when I returned home. I was an inveterate giggler and consequently received the 'strap' two or three times a week as punishment. It never worked so I learned very early that corporal punishment is totally ineffective. In later life I had to learn to laugh on the inside and not let it show – quite a difficult skill to master. I remember using a slate and chalk at infant school and this was really good because you could rub off your mistakes. The trouble was the chalk made a lot of dust and you went home covered in white powder.

Those were the days when parents supported teachers. If I returned home and said I had been in trouble, I then received another telling off from my parents. How times have changed. Now if a child goes home and says they have been in trouble inevitably the parents will come to the school and the teacher will surely be in the firing line. What a lot the parents of today have to learn about finding out all parts of a story before they jump in with both feet!

I did quite well at school but I was not particularly brilliant. My father had a very negative attitude toward school and me. When I was not in the top three of the class he was annoyed. He was mortified the time I came eighth out of forty and made me do extra homework for a year to regain my position. He would always be extremely proud of me when chatting to his friends and boast of my achievements, but never did he praise me personally. If I went out somewhere and made an effort to get dressed up he would always comment on something negative such as 'the seam in your stocking is not quite straight' or 'your hair is sticking up at the back.' I think he himself felt inferior for some reason and to keep ahead of the family, he felt he had to put us down. My mother suffered the same treatment and I do not know how she coped.

So began a complex that has stayed with me my whole life, not eased by gaining two degrees and endless postgraduate diplomas etc. Eventually, after receiving advice from a very good counsellor I recognised the problem, realised I did not have to be continually achieving and became happier with myself.

When shopping with my mother I recall her handing over the ration books for various goods. Then, butter was cut from a huge, cylindrical bright yellow pat on the counter. The sugar and various other dried foods were weighed out of barrels and put into blue paper bags. When bottles of juices etc were empty they were taken back to the shop and a few pennies deducted from the bill. This eliminated the waste and fancy packaging that now needs endless coloured receptacles so it can be recycled. I recall the foul smelling fly papers that hung from the ceilings to kill off the flies. I would always be bought some chocolate buttons as a treat, but no junk food existed in those days. Fruit was available only in season. We waited until Christmas for oranges and every summer when the strawberries appeared I used to come out in a nettle rash. We shopped on a main road, a short walk away from our home and I was terrified whenever I heard the tanks approaching. The Vickers Armstrong factory sent their tanks to be tested to the west of Newcastle and they had to come along the main shopping road out of the city. As they neared, the road began to shake and the gigantic rumbling made me hide in my mother's skirts with her hands over my ears.

Christmas was a wonderful and magic time. Decorations and baubles were in short supply after the war so my father made a selection of tree ornaments that I still have almost sixty years later. My mother and I sat and made paper streamers and pinned them up. Each year we had a goose for Christmas dinner and I can still smell the bitter aroma as my grandfather singed the feathers and dressed the bird. The very long quill feathers were shaped into nibs and used to write with. My favourite treat was a Christmas visit to Fenwick's toy department in Newcastle. The magical moving window displays transported children from cold and dark winter days to another land. The toy department was wonderful. Many years later I had enormous pleasure in taking my own children to this toy display.

Living with grandparents had ups and downs. I benefited from being spoiled by so many people but my parents did not have the freedom needed to really be themselves. My grandparent's house had a large 'drawing' room that was only used in the evenings and on special occasions. When my grandmother was out I would go into this room and my mother would play nursery rhymes on the piano for me or she would put a record on the huge gramophone, wind it up, and we would sing to it then run to wind it up again before it slowed down. I used to watch at the window for the 'Rington's Tea' horse and cart to arrive. We went out to buy provisions and I was lifted up and allowed to stroke the huge velvet nose of the lovely soft Shire horse. The gardeners came out with a bucket and spade to gather the droppings for their gardens. At night times there was a lovely coal fire in the drawing room. I would peep out of the window and see the lamplighter come and light the gas street lamps.

A sudden and unexplainable sadness penetrated my happy days in 1953 on American Independence Day. I was seven years old. My grandfather had suffered with stomach ulcers all his life. He travelled to London hospitals for many operations but was never fully cured. As he retired he went into the General Hospital in Newcastle and I was taken to visit him. I did not recognise the old, weary man who tried so hard to smile at me. I was given special dispensation to visit because children were not allowed on wards in the 1950's. After one evening visit my mother and father returned home and went into the drawing room with my grandmother. I peeked through the keyhole and saw my mother and grandmother crying. I had never seen my mother cry and it scared me. She was just 28 years old, very pretty and lively. Now she looked ghastly. My father came into the sitting room and told me that my grandfather had gone to live with Jesus. I wanted to know why he could not come back and live with us again. I did not receive a satisfactory answer. Many miserable days passed when everyone had very long faces. Then a major feast appeared on the table, there was much 'to-ing and fro-ing' and my mother and father went out and returned with lots of the family. This was clearly the funeral tea. My grandmother did not go as it was the custom in the North-East that wives often did not attend. I thought it was very peculiar all these people talking about my granddad and what he had done. It was years before any one explained funerals to me. All I knew was that I had seen him in the hospital, from where he went to live with Jesus. This did nothing to reinforce my negative perception of hospitals and I thought this Jesus man was pretty cruel taking my beloved granddad from me.

Winters in the fifties were perishing cold in the North-East. On some November days I recall going to school with my mother and having to hold on to the garden walls at the side of the path because the dank fog was so thick it was impossible to see for more than a few yards. I disliked these fogs as they brought an uneasy eeriness with them and, when walking, a shape would suddenly startle me out of the shadows and both parties would get a fright. The fogs also made us cough and splutter and I had to wear a scarf around my mouth. From December to February the weather was freezing and I recall very deep snow, although since I was only small it may not have been as deep as I thought. Houses were heated with coal fires that were built up before retiring and when they went out that was it, with no more heating until they were lit again the next morning. I had a round, stone hot water bottle in my bed and when I awoke each morning I used to see if 'Jack Frost' had visited. This meant that the insides of the windows were frozen solid and patterned with the water droplets that had frozen into a myriad of shapes.

Overall my main childhood memories are of warm summer sunshine and very little rain, of playing with friends in safe communities, of exploring the countryside and when we moved to our own home, of helping my father in his immaculate and prolific garden. We never visited a greengrocer as everything was grown for us according to the season. In summer, salads were picked as desired and tasted superb. In winter, vegetables were good and strong and turned into heart-warming soups. Slowly but surely the number of cups won for garden produce grew.

As I mentioned earlier, my parents gaily spent the money they had been given to buy a house when they were married. Part of it went on lovely annual holidays at a very comfortable hotel at Troutbeck in the Lake District run by the Guest family, which we all loved. It had everything from cream teas in the garden, surrounding fells to walk and plenty of animals to watch. We travelled there on a super bus with thick plush seats that I hated because they felt all scratchy on the back of my legs and they had a distinctive dusty smell. The bus stopped half way there at a little village called Alston and everyone got out and had a cup of tea. When all were replete we set off again. Time was *our* master in those days. My memories are indicative of how society has changed. For example, I must have been about eight when I looked out of the bus window to see a huge bull and cow copulating for all to see. When I asked, quite innocently, "Mummy, why is that cow trying to climb on its friend" a pair of hands was placed over my eyes and I was told it was a 'naughty bull'. Rather different to today, what?

One summer, we played cricket with the other guests and I was the wicket keeper. That soon changed as I was knocked out with the bat and woke up some time later. However, no suing for compensation then, just a large glass of fresh, home made lemonade, a cold bandage and on with the game. Such behaviour, I am sure, taught me just to accept life's little knocks, get up, and get on with it. Margaret Thatcher would have been proud of me.

We were the first in our street to get a television, for the Coronation. This was a huge monstrous piece of furniture with a tiny screen that completely filled a large corner of the room. It chirped and crackled and snowed regularly and showed us people in black and white who spoke English as I had not heard it before. All the family crowded in to watch. Later in my life when coloured television became the norm, I never ever forgot the thrill of switching on to see such brilliant colours after watching the world in black and white during my formative years.

My parents were very kind, proud and straight-laced people – 'sex' to them was what you carried coal in. They rarely showed affection to each other or to me and I never heard them argue. I cannot remember my mother ever receiving a bunch of flowers, except those from the garden and a box of chocolates only ever appeared at Christmas. They had a strong, old-fashioned work ethic. My mother had to remain the dutiful wife and mother at home until I went to grammar school. My father was the breadwinner and the boss. I saw my mother frustrated on many occasions but she never let it show, she simply got her head in a book and read herself out of her depression. My parents even switched off the television if someone began kissing.

Some of my childhood memories are lost on this generation. For instance, I used to love running out of the house when the sweep came, to watch his swirly brush peek out of the top of the chimney. Also, I remember being taken to the Quayside in Newcastle to see the ships. The Tyne was a working river then.

The Quayside was dark and moody; buildings were grimy and blackened with the smoke from the ships' funnels. The seafarers seemed exciting, loud, rough men with coarse beards and big arms covered in tattoos that told of their adventures. Of course, this was a place one could only go with parents and with strict instructions not to speak to anyone. Such a shame, what stories they all could have told!

As a child in the fifties the main entertainments were uniformed organisations such as Brownies and Guides and I loved these. I remember the thrill of burning cakes to get a cookery badge and of nearly setting fire to the local church hall when being tested for camp craft. Instead of discos we had Scottish country dancing, barn and ballroom dancing, activities that lent themselves well to getting held around the waist by boys.

I remember from very early in my childhood strange things happening that were simply dismissed by my mother. For example, one day as we sat in my grandmother's drawing room a large Edwardian mirror literally jumped from its hooks above the fireplace, stayed on the mantelpiece for a few seconds, then fell face down on the floor. Not a scratch on it. My mother simply said, "Oh, dear, something has happened to your great granddad". We discovered later that he had, in fact, died. He had given the mirror to my mother. Following my grandfather's death I told my mother that he had been to see me during the night. I know he had, I saw him. She did not dispute the fact, simply told me that the dead do not hurt us, only the living. I was to learn later in life that she had a psychic part to her character that I had seemingly inherited.

The only really unhappy times in my young life were when my mother seemed to have terrible rages for no reason at all. The slightest thing startled her and often I would receive a good hard smacking that left nasty bruises. Goodness knows what the child protection teams of today would have made of it. Of course in later life I realised she was going through the 'change.' She had to have a hysterectomy before she was forty, which solved the problems for her. A very manly lady surgeon, who brought her pet Alsatian to consultations, looked after my mother. The dog either scared the patients into submission, or if like my mother they loved dogs, it was very relaxing for them.

When I entered grammar school my mother went to work. She was an intelligent, well-read lady and totally unchallenged as a housewife. After working as a catering manager for a while she entered the civil service, quickly becoming an executive officer. When she retired, just as she looked forward to some great experiences, she had to look after her mother who had developed Alzheimer's.

Going to grammar school was hard, because in those days we were separated from our friends – the academic to the grammar and others equally talented to the secondary modern. Many secondary modern pupils are now creative millionaire entrepreneurs and many grammar pupils solid managerial people, usually in banks or teaching.

Our teachers were okay really. Those who were enthusiastic about their subject influenced us in our choice of what to study. Even at this age I realised the impact teachers had on young people's lives. Of course, there were always a few male teachers who felt females should be subservient and tried to turn them into quivering jellies every time they opened their mouths. As a consequence, I have hated mathematics all my life and never forgiven the b★★★★★★ who taught it!

Two major events stick out in my memory of school. The first was the time when a teacher suffered a heart attack and died in his chair during an assembly and the curtains had to be closed on the stage to hide the terrible sight. He had been going to marry the domestic science teacher and, though they were both middle-aged, it was a love story that had engaged the hearts of the pupils, so everyone was saddened greatly by his death.

The second was the time when, whilst a member of a school party visiting Cannes, we waited for a plane at Nice airport for ages only to be told that it had crashed on the way over carrying a party of schoolboys. We were then transported through the Alps by bus to Geneva to board a plane for Newcastle. To say the plane was old would be complementing it. Outside toilets would have been a luxury. As we flew home we encountered an electrical storm and the plane dropped dramatically, as did our stomachs. Believe me, when I stepped from that aeroplane in Newcastle onto terra firma I vowed never to get on a plane again and I did not relent that vow for forty years.

Being a musician, I was in the church choir and the school choir and I joined in the productions of various Gilbert and Sullivan operas. This was great fun and kept me out of trouble. Going into the teenage years was fantastic, after all these were the sixties. What liberation there was for a generation previously held within strict the confines imposed by war-time. Fashion for us females was very full skirts with huge net petticoats to make them stand out and wide belts to make the waist look slimmer. This was accessorised by hairstyles that a swarm of bees could make their nest in and shoes with stiletto heels that caused serious damage to anyone whose toes were stepped on accidentally. 'Jukebox Jury,' a hugely popular television record show, brought pop music into the lounge. We all had huge and ungainly reel-to-reel tape recorders and recorded really awful quality songs that we danced to all week. Everyone had hula-hoops and used them faithfully to make sure waist measurements were no more than 24 inches. I have to tell you they worked.

We began to experience strange feelings in areas of our bodies we did not talk about when boys were around. Those in our year groups were great as friends but were still the spotty mortals they had always been. However, the hunks in the sixth form, they were a different matter. They had to shave and some were even growing side-burns like Elvis, until told to remove them by masters.

My parents wanted me to remain a little girl for as long as possible so stockings and high heels were out until I was fourteen. I remember one day stealing my mother's stockings and putting them on. Feeling like a million dollars, I walked along to the local shop just to be mortified half way along the road when they began to wrinkle and fall around my knees. I did not realise they only stayed up with the help of a suspender belt. The embarrassment was acute.

School dances were a hot bed for meeting the opposite sex and when other schools were invited the talent grew admirably. Have you ever done the twist, bopped with a friend and taken in all the talent in the room at the same time? Not easy, but it was possible. Then you had to master the art of kissing without sounding like a sink plunger and breaking a nose on the way in. Oh, and what was this revolting thing that was being pushed down your throat by the other person involved? Only when you were totally bowled over by the other person did you allow tongues to wrap around each other because it usually resulted in having to steady yourself, as your legs wouldn't work with the power of the experience.

All of us experimented with the make-up available, which was precious little. We brightened our hair with lemon juice and made it shine by rinsing it with beer – very effective. Cucumber slices brightened our eyes and old English rose petals made lovely scent. Who says today's youth know all the answers.

This was the time when self-consciousness was at a premium and, having watched a recent generation of youngsters go through the same ritual, little has really changed. Each sex still remains at the edge of the hall, they look each other up and down all evening, chatter excitedly about who they fancy and then, as the evening ends, they decide to communicate.

Having a 'steady' was an accomplishment and most of us managed it by the sixth form. Then we took our steady to parties – wild parties. Here we had to learn the knack of keeping them interested without giving them what they invariably wanted – for free love was not quite established. When his hand stroked your leg and made its way slowly to the top of your stockings you had to learn not to gasp out loud with pleasure but to show how you disapproved of such a gesture and he had to hide his obvious excitement with a long jacket.

Occasionally accidents happened and someone got caught out. At this time such an action was considered an absolute catastrophe. Can you imagine the kafuffle when your pretty, auburn haired friend became pregnant in the sixth form? Well, she did a disappearing act from school and we were not allowed to speak to her if we called or rang. Teachers' would not answer questions about her departure and her family moved to another part of the country. No one ever heard from her again. Thank goodness things have changed.

Whilst in the sixth form I went to the local church one evening and listened to a very handsome young man take the service. I was told he had a steady girlfriend, so that thought had to fly out of the window. I was so naïve then! Mind, whilst he delivered the sermon I had a few dreams of being in this tall, dark and handsome man's arms and wow was my face red.

During the Easter holiday of the same year I decided to go on a weekend youth activity organised by the Church since there was precious little else to do. I met my friends and we made our way to the meeting point in the city to get the bus – very few people had cars in those days you know. We dutifully queued up. On we got and I was in trouble, because I had been suffering from a throat infection for weeks and found speaking difficult. Imagine a 17 year old girl who could not speak – I expect if any men should ever read this their comment will be 'fantastic', as a woman without a voice is probably their idea of heaven. This condition was actually caused by nerves at the forthcoming 'A' level examinations. These were, as the words say, examinations lasting three to four hours each. No coursework then.

As I sat on the bus a tall, dark young man leaned over and spoke to me. I turned around and it was the one I had listened to in the church. Close up he was much better looking and he smelled nice too. He had the most gorgeous, melting brown eyes and a lovely smile. I was smitten. Only I couldn't say anything and everyone else was chatting him up fast. Ah well I thought, that's life.

We stayed at a majestic, historical hall in Northumberland and, miracle of miracles, this lovely young man followed me around. He had just finished with a girlfriend and lots of her pals were there, so they kept a very close watch on me and very loudly whispered how she could get him back anytime she liked. Well, I had always liked a challenge so I nudged up to him and tried my best to charm him without words.

The problem was that I was due to meet someone else over the weekend who I had been seeing for a few weeks. However this tall, dark and handsome young man was here and now, charming, well mannered and full of charisma. I did a terrible thing and dumped the lad I had been seeing. In later years I often wondered what happened to the poor young man I so unceremoniously discarded. I have had many twinges of shame for the ungracious and undignified way I treated him and wish I could have been able to apologise properly.

I paid the price for being with one of the most coveted and popular chaps at the conference. One evening when walking in through the door a whole bucket of water landed on me, thrown from the battlements to hit him but he moved and I copped it. How I laughed, even though I was soaking wet and freezing cold – after all I couldn't let him think I didn't have a sense of humour could I?

Then, another evening, I found this young man had a wicked sense of humour and a limitless fount of jokes, something that has never changed all his life. As we walked romantically along a really black country lane with owls hooting and lambs bleating, he told me a really hilarious joke. I laughed so loudly I proceeded to disgrace myself mightily by adding to the evening sounds, as the wind broke free during the laugh. I laughed at his joke; he fell about laughing at me, so the ice was well and truly broken.

During this weekend he told me he loved me and I was very uncertain of what to do next as this was new territory for me.

However, I did melt into nothingness when he held me tight and those places that were beginning to make themselves known to me began to ache for something I had never experienced before.

At first I hid his existence from my parents as he was six years older than me and they would not, I knew, approve. What was even worse, he rode a motorbike. Now this was an absolute 'no-no' as far as my folks were concerned. They had high aspirations for me and would not take kindly to what they considered an 'older' man on a motorbike getting in the way, even though he was a well-qualified engineer. However, this young man was nothing if not determined. He was having none of this and roared up one evening, unannounced, on his motorbike. He charmed them but they still were not totally happy, so quite a few surreptitious meetings had to be organised until they gave in, seeing I was determined to stay with him.

Many times I would be walking home from school and a motorbike would roar up and there he was. It was very infra-dig to have a boyfriend who was older and at work when in the sixth form. He used to like seeing me in school uniform with knee-high socks. He played romantic records for me and told me he loved me so many times I just had to believe it. This was not a time of political correctness, in fact anything but. However, my young man was the essence of charm, courtesy and good manners and I was treated like someone who really mattered. It made me feel great and never cost me a penny.

When my A level results were due my lack of confidence took over and I simply had not the nerve to collect them and in those days they were not given by phone. I had to write a letter authorising the school to hand the results to my boyfriend and he returned with them. Luckily they were excellent and any worries dispersed with the celebrations.

We spent many warm and wonderful evenings going for long walks along the coast or sitting at the mouth of the Tyne, imagining our life together as we watched the sun set in a pinky haze. For us there were only two people in the world and we were invincible.

The next big move for me was college in the autumn of 1964. I did not go too far away from home. My choice was Neville's Cross College which was part of the University of Durham. Since few people had cars then I was far enough from my parents to be totally independent. This was to be the first and final move from my childhood home because I needed my independence and freedom and I wanted to see the world outside the North-East. My young man, Henry, was at that time a marine engineer waiting to go to Westminster Theological College in Cambridge and often he skipped work and sped on his motorbike to my college to see me. I skipped lectures and off we would go. The only problem was that I kept falling asleep on the pillion and as he cornered he had to fight hard to keep the bike upright.

He played the drums in a group and was busy gigging most weekends, so I could have a good time at College as well as having my cake during the week. Little did I know that drumming in bands brought groupies and that could lead to other problems.

At this time LSD was common and it was easy in university circles to obtain drugs of all shapes and sizes, but I was never really interested. I saw what LSD did to some of my friends. The trips they went on were often horrific and I decided I did not wish to join them.

Of course, I had to be introduced to Henry's family. Now, I didn't know then that a sprig of garlic or body armour might have been useful before such an introduction. His brother, sisters and father were lovely, welcoming and kind but his mother was something else. The name 'Attila the Hun' comes to mind. On my very first meeting, because I was so much younger than Henry she accused him of 'baby snatching' in front of the whole family. I learned to live with the snide comments, the usual 'not good enough for my son' remarks and the horrendous rudeness aimed at bringing me down 'a peg or two'.

I learned how not to be a mother-in-law from her. I dreaded the invitations to 'afternoon tea'. She had such airs and graces, such delusions of grandeur because her father had owned a brickworks and built her house and yet here she was, serving chunky bread and jam at tea.

Sixties summers were warmed with free love, great music, life under the stars and very youthful passionate feelings. When Henry went to Cambridge he would race back North to my college on exeat weekends and demand I had a scarf ready for his neck to warm him up-I leave it to your imagination to decide what he could have meant by this!

Henry was definitely a 'leg man.' In those days I really did have lovely legs – they went all the way to the ground you know. I am still trying to find the remnants of them in what I now call legs. Those meetings were very intense and fabulous – wild and mind blowing. I remember his liquid brown eyes begging me for more and I just dissolved into helplessness. His words matched his eyes, I felt the most important person in the world, in his world.

I was almost always faithful at college and only once nearly strayed with a rugby player who took me to a party at the men's college. It was a great night and we went on to Lumley castle afterwards. Everyone was happy and pairing off for fun and games and the opportunity was there. But I didn't take it as I cared far too much for my young man to want to be with anyone else. Others may have had their cake and eaten slices from other tables, but that was not for me.

Students were lucky in the sixties as tuition and accommodation was paid for, we only had to sort out money for general living and books. I worked through the summer and winter vacations. In the summer I spent my time, with many other students, on the production line in a sweet factory watching fruit pastilles go into packets day after day. It was so mind and foot numbing that I would often walk the four miles home each evening to kick start my feelings. In the winter I worked night shift at the central post office in Newcastle, sorting parcels. This certainly improved my geography. Occasionally if funds were desperate I would work in Boots on Saturdays during term time, but this was usually just for special expenditure. I feel so desperately sorry for young people at university nowadays having to borrow to survive, what kind of a start in life is this?

Teaching practices at college reassured me that this was the right choice of career for me. I was sent into the wilds of Durham on one practice into a hard working little mining village, whose inhabitants spoke with very strong accents and were difficult to understand. Here coal was delivered to miners' houses and to the school and left in huge piles at the gates. A corner of the school playground was cordoned off and the caretaker carried the coal inside creating a black mountain that kept the school fires burning. Local mothers wore their daily uniform as they cooked and cleaned – scarves rolled into turbans around their hair and 'pinny's' (sort of overalls with flowers on). They had dresses for Sundays and special days.

In the classroom, the teacher's table and chair were in the corner in front of the fire – yes, the coal fire! Imagine what health and safety would make of it now. The poor children at the far corner of the room were freezing but the teacher had a round, warm and glowing posterior all day. No accidents had ever been reported and the teacher kept the fire built up all day. At this time the boys in junior schools wore short trousers and I recall them coming in each winter morning with legs that were various shades of blue and pink from the bitter winds, hoping to thaw out before the fire as the register was taken.

On a second practice I was sent to Bishop Auckland to a secondary school and told to teach scripture to classes of pupils aged between twelve and fifteen. The teacher gave me no notes or ideas, just disappeared to have a cup of tea and I was left to survive. The pupils were, to say the least, tough. They wanted to know if I had a boyfriend, how far would I go with him and other facts in this vein. I have to say they were not much interested in the Old Testament. So I ditched my carefully planned lesson notes and we talked about how parents had favourites amongst their families and gradually I introduced the story of Joseph.

This experience taught me that you have to interest children at their level and begin at their starting point if you are going not only to survive the experience, but also be successful and extend their knowledge and understanding of the subject and the world around them. I also realised I preferred to teach the younger children.

During these practices we had to teach a range of subjects and I gleaned two very useful and practical tips, from lecturers who were old hands at the job, that are as pertinent today as they were then. The first was not to talk above a tape in games or dance lessons as children cannot concentrate on two conflicting voices at once and you lose their attention. The second was that when teaching the youngest children tell a story without using the book. I soon realised that the inflections in my voice as I dramatised fear, excitement etc and my gestures absorbed children's attention more than following pictures. It is a difficult skill but worth working at. My friends and I had great fun back at college telling stories to a tape recorder and listening to ourselves. I have passed these tips to many young and inexperienced teachers and they have improved more lessons than I care to mention.

These were the days when, in addition to academic disciplines, we were taught the basics of teaching at College. We learnt how to teach children to speak correctly, how to use a mirror to help them form vowel shapes accurately, how to teach them to write and how to teach phonics without making a total mess of the sounds ourselves. Believe me it was pretty hard going. Some of the schools we went to were in staunch Geordie pit villages where the language did not in any way resemble English. We had trouble deciphering it, never mind trying to change the way children spoke it.

Another pet hate of the lecturers we had was the incorrect pronunciation of sounds. Boy, we sure were told off if we made mistakes and our marks were downgraded. For example, we were told categorically that there is no such sound as 'suh', the letter 's' is pronounced 'ss' as in hiss. Actually the lecturers were right, it makes learning to read so much easier for children if they have an accurate knowledge of phonic sounds and blends.

At this time, I had my first experience of just what a charmer my boyfriend was and of the girls littering his past. A former girlfriend of his appeared at a college dance we went to in Cambridge. Her friends kept asking Henry to dance with her for 'old time's sake.' He asked what I thought and I said it was unacceptable, so he refused to dance with her. If you are a man reading this you will be wondering what all the fuss is about and why, for goodness sake, can a woman not realise that you can have lots of relationships at different levels all at the same time. If you are a woman you will, I believe, know that the way that men think bears no resemblance to the way women think and agree that this woman was trying to assert her influence and show me up. Correct?

In my last year at college, on my twenty-first birthday Henry and I got engaged. He presented me with a beautiful ruby and diamond ring and we were deliriously happy. We celebrated at a gorgeous restaurant in Durham in the Bridge Hotel. It was olde world, dark and romantic. My mother was furious, she thought I was throwing my life away but I was far too happy to care. Henry's crabby old mother simply said my ring was 'pretty' and very little more. When you are young and in love only two people matter and nothing could spoil our joy.

CHAPTER 2

Stepping Out

After finishing at college I received job offers from three counties surrounding Cambridge. I turned them down as I wanted a job within the City in order to be nearer Henry. I applied for a post in a city school and was successful. I moved to a small furnished bed-sit in Devonshire Road, on the first floor of a house owned by an old lady. I was an acceptable lodger because I was a teacher. Henry was allowed to visit because he was a theological student. I did not spoil the old lady's vision of theological students, better to let her believe they were clean and good.

Time passed and we were married in Newcastle on the 23rd December, 1967, at the end of my first term teaching. My parents had to organise everything and there were no emails then. Henry had grown a beard at college, much to the dismay of both sets of parents. The night before the wedding, as a joke, he shaved half of it off. He came to my house and sat with his hand over half of his face, then changed his hand and my parents were mystified. First they saw a beard, and then they didn't! My father didn't have an electric razor so Henry had to see the minister and go for stag night drinks with half a beard, much to the amusement of his friends.

The morning of the wedding dawned. Our respective homes were far apart so we did not see each other before we arrived at the church. Henry's morning had been somewhat spoiled, however. A few weeks earlier he was drumming in a swanky London nightclub in order to earn money for our honeymoon. On the way back to Cambridge, at three in the morning, he put his foot down, thinking the road was deserted. The inevitable blue light appeared and pulled him over.

When the policeman discovered he was a theological student he made some very sarcastic remarks. As Henry drove away he commented to the policeman, "When I'm qualified I'll be happy to marry your parents". Not a good idea, as we found out when the summons and fine were delivered on the wedding morning. He has never again been pulled up for speeding. Sadly the same does not apply to me. We had a romantic Christmas wedding, with snowflakes falling as we came out of the church. I had long johns hidden away beneath a designer dress to keep me warm. We were very, very happy. Friends invited us to spend our honeymoon with them and we drove in a dream across the snowy Pennines to their home.

As we stopped for a call of nature the snow was falling heavily, so we collected umbrellas and made our way to a local hotel in a pretty village. On opening the umbrellas confetti tumbled out and made a rainbow of colours on the white snow, much to the local's amusement. Our faces were redder than the confetti. Our friends in Liverpool looked after us fantastically well.

Our parents said we were mad to get married at Christmas but we were young and didn't listen as love was all that mattered. Later in life we agreed with them. We were rarely free of church obligations at Christmas and never able to celebrate as we wished. If the remote possibility occurred that we were free, we could never afford the extortionate prices charged at that time of year.

In Cambridge there was no engineers' salary and no student grant, just my newly qualified teacher's salary, which was a pittance. We used my savings to furnish our home. Sadly, Henry's faithful old jalopy gave up the ghost and was replaced by two ancient squeaky bicycles that kept us very fit.

My flat had been for one person, so we were house hunting again. We eventually found a place in York Street, close to the railway, at the princely sum of £3 a week. This was not cheap, but was the usual rent for a two up, two down with back yard and outside loo. Henry's college did not have married accommodation because they did not approve of married students. Thank goodness things have changed. We were happy in this tiny house with our faithful black and white cat. We had no bathroom. Difficult, but we managed. Youth and love can cope with virtually anything. We either used a tin bath in front of the fire or I sneaked into Henry's strict all male college and got into the enormous baths they had, with him. We certainly enjoyed that very much, I can tell you.

The whole house was warmed by a coal fire in the tiny sitting-room. Our cat frequently performed a death-defying walk across the mantle-piece, in and out of the ornaments, looking at us with a very wicked grin on her face. She never, ever knocked anything over but this did nothing to soothe our nerves as we watched the performance. We were happy, penniless and in love. We had the freedom that only comes with new and young love, no responsibilities and a beautiful city to live in. On Friday evenings wives could eat in the college. This was a super meal. It was free, kept our stomachs replenished until Sunday and helped stretch out the housekeeping. It was the same for all the married students.

I worked happily at St. Matthew's primary school in the middle of Cambridge. It was a smashing little school with a very happy staff team. The junior building was new with lots of wood and weird shaped roofs that were rather like cheese wedges. In the winter they leaked all over the shop and buckets had to be placed strategically in the classrooms. An elderly head mistress, Miss Franklin, ran the school rather like an extended family. She had a beautiful silvery white bun and was the epitome of a village headmistress, with her voluminous skirts and rimmed spectacles that sat precariously on the end of her nose. We in the juniors hardly ever saw her. Perhaps it would be fairer to say she 'appeared' elderly to us, as we were young and just qualified and she was nearing retirement. We never dreamt that one day we could possibly be that age. Never. Not us!

The head mistress chose to have her office in the infants building. This was an older and warmer building with many helpers to make her cups of tea and generally look after her. We didn't mind, it was great to be free of management. Miss Franklin expected staff to dress smartly. Smart teachers, she maintained, showed they respected their pupils. She was quire right of course. Even now teachers in tight tracksuit bottoms that show they could balance a pile of books on their behinds aggravate me intensely. Miss Franklin made sure we planned our work thoroughly and made our rooms colourful and interesting. At the time we groaned about her demands but it was all good training.

I made two very good friends here, Jennifer and Joy. Jennifer's husband was at Ridley House (the Anglican college), so we had similar lives and Joy had immigrated to Britain from Pakistan. Her parents had fled Albania and begun a missionary hospital in Lahore. She was a fascinating person and made curries for us that tasted better than any we have had before or since.

I was responsible for a small class of eight year olds with a good mix of abilities. I also trained the choir, the recorder groups and organised the concerts. If it was musical, I did it. I had many happy times with groups performing at the Guildhall and loved it. If you have musical talent you may in time hide it as I did, otherwise you organise every concert, show and performance and all your breaks, lunch hours and after school times are taken up with rehearsals. The tension grows, kids are absent and you race around like the proverbial fly trying to fill gaps and improvise the costumes that mothers forgot to send. After the performance you can, of course, glow in the glory of it all but you reach a time when you ask if this is worth so much of your time. Often it is not, but what is worth the effort is the pride and pleasure on the children's faces as they perform. One advantage of being responsible for music is that it can offer you opportunities to meet a wide range of people and gain skills in addition to those required in the classroom.

Parents of the children in my class were from all walks of life, teaching, lecturing, local business folk, and a few students. The children were a cosmopolitan blend that fed from each other and were very stimulating to teach. I did laugh one day, however, when a very happy Italian boy came back to school after a short absence. At registration he duly presented his note and on opening, it I read the reason for his absence. It read,

Dear Mrs Gordon,
Carlo has been absent from school as he had a bad dose of dirrrxxxxx, dareeeexxxxx, dxxxxxxxx – a bad does of the shits!

English is a hard language and the word his mother wanted was very difficult to spell so she reverted to good old Anglo-Saxon. This was nearly as good as the note my father-in-law had received from one of his parents –

Dear Teacher,
Johnny was off as he had the shits through a hole in his boot.

This was from a parent in the toughest part of Newcastle just off Scotswood Road, where survival was the main object of the day. In this school there was no playground and the teacher rang the bell in the surrounding 'back lanes' to gather the children at the beginning of the morning and afternoon.

I quickly realised that diplomacy was an essential skill for a teacher. In one of the first pieces of written work I marked I was presented with the narrative-'Daddy was away working so Uncle James came round to keep us company. Mummy was cold so Uncle James kept her warm in bed. Mummy does not want daddy to worry, so I have not got to tell him about it.' I praised the child because the spellings were good and I quietly removed it from the book. From my first week of teaching to my last, I have always been thrilled when children grasped an idea or became engrossed in an aspect of learning. It was and still is wonderful to literally 'see' them learn as their faces show the pleasure they gain at achieving.

For a while, I experienced a lot of stomach-ache. The doctor sent me to the New Addenbrookes hospital for a barium enema.

Little did I know what was about to happen. Henry was very concerned so he rode with me to the hospital. As it was, nothing serious was wrong. Having had the enema and the x-ray, I decided I would never have another and was told I could go home. Neither of us realised that the effects of an enema can last for a few hours. In our naivety we began the ride home, on our rickety bicycles, about three or four miles. After ten minutes I was desperate and I sped off ahead of Henry who, along with a few motorists, could not keep up with me. I hopped into Homerton College to dispose of the remnants of the enema. By the time he caught up I was fine. I have never kept up with him, let alone be ahead of him, since.

One Christmas in Cambridge Henry had a really bad bout of gastro-enteritis. He looked grey, felt green and did not seem to be making any progress. Rather, he was getting progressively worse. The doctor would not come out to him. Things haven't changed much in forty years, have they? I kept ringing and insisted the doctor visited as Henry had a terrible cough and was very dehydrated. Eventually the doctor arrived. He was very angry at being called to a student, after all students were insignificant creatures, a pain in the neck and irresponsible. So when our mischievous young cat decided to do a wall of death around the house, finally racing up the stairs and straight up the doctor's leg, sharp needle claws fully extended, I thoroughly enjoyed watching his face go red and contort, racked with pain. It paid him back for his bad attitude and earned the cat a special fish supper. Cats are wonderful creatures; they are funny, independent and give masses of affection. However, they regard their owners as their 'staff' and soon lay down the house rules about how they wish to be cared for. The odd thing is that owners obey these rules.

I must admit we had the best of both worlds in Cambridge. I was working at a job I loved, Henry was studying for a vocation he felt called to and we had fun being part of university life. Henry played the drums for the Footlights club and backed many folk who are now household names in the entertainment world.

He was an extremely good drummer and had the chance to become professional, but he turned it down. How different our life together may have been had he chosen that route.

His only difficulty was reading music as he drummed. On one occasion he was needed to accompany a production of 'Oh, what a Lovely war' at the Arts theatre, starring Germaine Greer. So that he read the score correctly, I sat in the orchestra pit and counted him in at the right spot and it was great fun.

The loveliest time in the city was springtime when the trees were heavy with pink and white baskets of blossom and the 'backs' were carpeted with myriad hues of yellow. Set against the bright blues skies of early spring, these stunning colours lifted the spirits upwards. We spent many warm spring afternoons walking along the backs, arm in arm in the sunshine, thinking life would always be as sunny. We had lots to learn.

Summer evenings were spent lazily lounging in a punt on the Cam and for most of the students, but thankfully not Henry, part of the evening was usually spent in the Cam. Cambridge is a very 'accepting and forgiving' city. It is tolerant of the idiosyncrasies and extravagances of youth, the eccentricities of academia of all ages and persuasions and the constant influx of the eager and camera hungry Japanese tourists, who block the paths as they get the right angle for their coveted photograph of King's Chapel. Comfortable seats in the bookshops encourage browsing, result in buying and lend a quiet and unreal atmosphere to the gleaming spires.

It was now 1968 and Henry's studies were coming to an end and the time drew near for us to move to a parish. Cambridge had been a sunny, warm companion to us but we were soon to feel the storms of change. My goodness, what a parish he was asked to go to – Toxteth, an inner city area of Liverpool that had a reputation for being deprived and violent. Can you imagine this timid, shy, well brought up 21 year old wife being put into the middle of 'Murder Mile' with her husband? To say it was a baptism of fire is a complete understatement.

CHAPTER 3

It's for Real, Folks

Our home in Toxteth was to be a large brick built, mid-terrace, double fronted Victorian house just off Smithdown Road. Actually, it was probably the best house we have ever had. It was huge with five bedrooms, four reception rooms, a butler's pantry, a well-appointed kitchen and an enormous bathroom with a huge self standing Victorian bath that was great fun. The only problem was the bathroom was so cold in winter that icicles hung from the pipes on the inside. The house was not centrally heated but had coal or gas fires in each room. We carpeted the parts we lived in and walked in slippers on bare floors around the rest. We could easily welcome the congregation, have meetings and still be completely private.

This move changed me from a wife and teacher to a non-person in one journey. I lost my name, my character, my identity. I became 'a clergy wife.' When attending functions I was not introduced as Mrs Gordon, rather as 'the minister's wife'. When I was asked to open fetes, I was welcomed and opened them as 'the minister's wife.'

As a clergy wife I learnt to walk one pace behind my husband, to sit on my own at functions and make polite conversation with everyone, whilst Henry was shepherded to the main table or the chair at the front of the meeting. I very quickly became competent in making small talk with people I would not otherwise have chosen to be with. I was adept at yawning without opening my mouth. I practised smiling benignly as I sat beside people I had never met before and who I would never see again after the function. I became skilful at nodding sweetly to everyone, whilst working out my lesson plans for the following week in my head.

I quite accept that there may be some wives for whom such an existence is supremely enjoyable and I greatly admire their ability to lose their personality and identity in such circumstances. But for me, well it was the beginning of little stirrings of dissent that grew into great storms of rage as I fought the confines and impositions of the church and its attempt to control me as well as Henry.

I was expected to be as holy as my husband, as prim, proper and refined as Jane Austen, as poor as the proverbial church mouse, as compassionate as Mother Theresa and to dress quietly and discreetly. I had to incorporate each of these personas in the small frame I had been blessed with. I really tried hard for a few months and then made a momentous decision. With Henry's support, I chose to be none of them. Had I known and understood the consequences of this choice, I may have had second thoughts.

We came to Liverpool, home of the Beatles, at the end of the sixties and we lived reasonably close to Penny Lane. Not that you would ever know it, because as soon as the council put the road sign up the fans stole it. Mini-skirts were in, or perhaps I would be more accurate in saying that some girls wore wide belts as skirts. On arrival here I too was a miniskirt wearer but that had to change. The perception of the congregation was that I would dress in tweeds and brogues. Although I compromised and lengthened my skirts I was never, ever, seen in tweeds and brogues from that day to this. I was also expected to wear a hat to church. Again I compromised and wore a fashionable 'Beatle' style cap, which Henry said gave me a 'cheeky little face.' This was deemed unsuitable by the old biddies in the pews. So I did not wear a hat in church from that day to this, except when I have chosen to wear one at special occasions.

I strongly supported Henry in his work. He was and still is a highly talented man whose ideas extend far beyond the staid institution of the church. He has an incredible pastoral gift that hundreds of people, both in and out of the church, have testified to on many occasions. He preached rip-roaring sermons that shook thoughts to the core, but such gifts were, over the years, to be slowly eroded or ignored by the institution he worked for.

For a while, as I made the transition to being myself, I still conformed to some clergy wife traditions. I attended church regularly, I raised money for the church and other charitable causes and I ran various organisations. I kept my burgeoning belief that the church was a staid, uninteresting and controlling institution to myself.

Our little black and white cat loved it here. She had great fun charging around the place, doing noisy war dances up and down the many stairs. We laughed a lot in this place and Henry's talents were appreciated by many of his flock. Because our house was so large we welcomed and accommodated students from around the world, clergymen from China and many friends from far and wide. We thoroughly enjoyed the richness they brought into our lives.

During this time Henry developed his ministry by playing the drums in local clubs. He helped many who would never enter the portals of the church, lending them an unconditional ear. His pastoral talents were exploited to the full and many non-church folk testified to the warmth that came from his ministry to them. The fees from the drumming also paid for happy holidays and little luxuries like bread and shoes.

It was not appropriate to accompany Henry when he played as he worked hard all night. This restricted my social life and I have regretted it often. For example, before we were in Liverpool each New Year we would celebrate the traditional Scottish way by attending a party, going first footing and ending up for breakfast at someone's house. This was great fun. In Toxteth we were so poor he had to play every New Year so socialising was out.

We bought a 'sensible' car here. It was an orange, 'Del Boy' Reliant Robin. Three wheels to our wagon and we were free.

Everyone laughed at use but it was all we could afford. We explored the countryside around Liverpool and had great fun. However, after Henry set it on fire one day when trying to repair it we decided to up the stakes and go for something with four wheels. Then I learned to drive. We could not afford lessons so Henry taught me. He is actually an excellent teacher. At this time he became an advanced driver, taught effectively by an off-duty police driver. His interest in driving has remained and recently he took a course offered by the local authority for the over 60's. This was probably, we think, arranged to get old age off the road and make it a safer place for younger speed merchants, however he obtained his ROSPA gold medal for driving proficiency and put paid to the notion that all older drivers are unfit.

Due to his good teaching I passed my test first time, much to his chagrin as it had taken him two attempts. I remember the sense of freedom when I went out on my own in the car for the first time – scared, yes, but free also and I still love driving. The car was broken into one evening and some church goods stolen. The men in the clubs where he played immediately raised the cash to replace the goods. Genuine generosity like this was very moving and an indication of how much they appreciated his care.

The people who lived in the area surrounding Smithdown Road were lovely if they were on top of things, but you did not annoy them if they were losing or you would never see your head again. They were hard working folk with 'lived in' faces. The dark, deep pencilled lines on their foreheads were trophies that demonstrated evidence of the stresses and strains they had experienced as they pushed and pummelled their way through a tough existence. Their tongues were sharp, sometimes coarse, often kindly and always to the point. They said what they thought without mincing their expressions. We found them to be generous and warm most of the time and very, very funny. For example, when standing at a bus stop an enormous funeral with masses of cars and flowers went past and, commenting to another person standing there that the deceased must have been popular,

Henry received the immediate answer, "I expect it was the social security man".

I remember helping out with the first wedding Henry conducted. This was arranged before our arrival so we did not know the couple. Everyone had arrived except the groom. The noise as the guests chattered loudly was rather like a market place. Some 'lit up' and had to be gently requested not to smoke. Their experience of churches was clearly limited. The groom's journey was longer than anticipated as the traffic was heavy on the road from Walton prison to the church. When the van arrived my eyes were on stalks as no one had told us the groom was in prison. He was a tough looking man with a scarred face and black teeth. The guards brought him in and demanded I lock the church door, as they did not want any escape attempts. He stood at the front of the church next to his bride with the prison officer alongside. They were handcuffed together throughout the service and those handcuffs never came off.

As the bride, groom and guard emerged from the service into the vestibule following the ceremony, the groom turned to the bride and said' Well, I hope you got what you wanted then'. He found it difficult kissing her as her 'bump' was rather large. He was taken, still shackled, back into the van and returned to his accommodation in Walton. The bride and her family went to the pub to celebrate. If a few chickens had run out of the church I would not have been surprised.

I also recall our first harvest festival with mixed feelings. We collected goods to distribute to the needy in the area, of whom there were many, and were astonished at the wealth of beautiful flowers by the harvest table. On closer scrutiny we noticed the 'black-fringed' greeting cards. The children had stolen them from the local cemetery. After dark, we had to slip into the cemetery and search for the graves to put them back

It was the duty of the 'clergy wife' to organise jumble sales. This was not a pleasant job. Sorting through the 'gifts' was a thankless task. Much went straight to the tip. I quickly learnt to wear rubber gloves when sorting. After all, can you imagine what it feels like to put your hand in a bag and pick out a pair of someone's dirty knickers? Believe me, it does not feel good. Even less pleasant was serving at the jumble sale. Henry used to look out of the door before the sale opened and shout, 'The diesel fitters are at the front of the queue again.' He was referring to the big, strong ladies who always managed to sneak to the front. These were ladies who had part-time jobs kick starting the jumbo jets at the airport. They showed incredible athleticism as they ran to the stalls and filled their bin bags with children's clothes, shouting 'dees'll fit our Jack, dees'll fit our Mary etc.' Hence their nickname the 'diesel fitters.' I never argued the price they offered; I valued my life too much.

The dealers also pushed in first and they were ruthless. They worked the jumble sale in pairs. One would ask a question while the other filled the bag below the counter. Then they would haggle for one purchase and leave with overflowing bags. The church members advised me not to tackle them and I took the advice readily.

Of course, I had to find work here. I went for interview at the local authority offices and was told one of the advisers had requested to see me as he had a suitable position that involved both class teaching and music. When I walked into his office, I was facing my old music teacher from grammar school. He had moved to the city as an adviser and had recognised my name. He said he had a job for me, it was tough, but he knew I could do it. He was right on all counts.

I was given the special needs junior class in a three-storey Victorian type school in Earle Road, just a few hundreds yards away from the church. The ground floor was the infants, the middle floor the juniors and the top floor the seniors. You may think this was primitive, but in the basement we had a swimming pool, so how avant-garde was this? On being appointed, I was shown my classroom by the head master who said, 'Now, dear, leave your door open and if we hear a riot we will come to help'.

The first morning I faced that mob of ruffians I decided it was them or me and it certainly was not going to be me. We quickly came to terms with each other, soon the children began to learn and make progress and I thoroughly enjoyed teaching them.

This was an old-fashioned classroom with high windows, so it rather resembled a large prison cell. I decorated it as brightly as I could because a stimulating environment really does have a positive impact on the children. Space was at a premium, so I quickly learned to have a neat desk and a neat room. Just as well as the head master told me that the sign of an efficient teacher is a clean desk. I labelled boxes for everything and ensured the children used them. I looked in the children's desks daily to make sure they were tidy.

I was so angry to see how these children had been thrown on the scrap heap at such a tender age. Often I would take shoes in for them but their parents would sell them the same night for drugs or drink. School was the only route available to these children to see the possibilities life could offer them so school had to be exceptionally effective.

I let the children know exactly what I would and would not tolerate from the very first moment I met them. I did not teach until we really understood each other's expectations. I showed them I was interested in them; I valued and supported them. I was never sarcastic because children, like the rest of us, hurt inside. They respond to praise like the rest of us and sarcasm can destroy them just as easily as it can destroy us. I worked out signals for behaviour and the children knew if they responded they had a star and so many stars meant a treat. These children had so little that it was not hard to find treats for them. Believe me, it was not easy and most nights I was shattered and felt all my energy had been drawn from me, but it was truly worth it. I learned that the secret of success was efficient preparation, organisation and high expectation. I felt the need to believe in these children and only want the best for them. I tried to make the material interesting and relevant to their needs, I gathered lots of resources for them and my expectations were high. Many of the children achieved and, after a while, some began to enjoy learning.

One morning a young boy began jumping around the tops of the desks on his arrival at school and I could see straight away he had been on drugs. Sadly, drugs were easily available in the area. His parents were addicts, they did not care for the child and he was well known to the authorities. I told the headmaster who arranged for social services to come for the child as he needed treatment. This resulted in me receiving death threats from the parents and needing a police escort home for a month. I was certainly seeing the seedier side of life. In the evenings I helped with the guide company at the church and, as I returned home one evening, a child jumped over a wall and cannoned into me with hands full of sweets and cigarettes having just broken into, and stolen from, the corner shop. He was in my class. I made him hand them back and apologise. On many occasions, my parents wondered what on earth Henry had taken me to.

I learned very quickly to hoard all kinds of things that could be used in the classroom. On the beach I picked up shells, in the woods I gathered cones. I would cut up old clothes into strips for collage, I asked the city shops for super items from their window displays when they changed them, as wonderful card and pictures and goodies were simply thrown into skips. I built up my own teaching materials and did not have to rely on non-existent school budgets. All teachers do this and attics around the country are full of boxes of bits and pieces that can be useful sometime.

A colleague in this school disliked teaching, having entered the profession primarily for the holidays and what they assumed to be a reasonably short working day. The profession treats such practitioners cruelly, is a heartless taskmaster and eventually breaks the spirit.

We ran a very popular youth club here that was well attended by some really lovely young people. They were disadvantaged simply because of where they lived. Many asked if they could use our address when applying for jobs, since their applications would immediately be discarded if they put their own addresses on their letter. We took them to a holiday centre in the Peak District and walked them until they couldn't stand up. Many of them had never seen farm animals; most had never been in the countryside. They mucked in, helped to cook, entertained themselves and were great fun to be with.

Henry moved to a neighbouring church in 1971 and we were provided with a comfortable home in a pleasant green area near Queen's Drive and things went well. This was quite an affluent church with many local dignitaries in the congregation, so again I was expected to play the typical clergy wife role. Many of the folk were lovely and they cared about each other, the community and us. One Sunday the Lord Mayor came in his coach that was drawn by four beautiful horses. Another Sunday the local clubs 'Pandemonium band' came dressed as clowns. They marched through the streets raising money for the work of the church in the area. There was never a dull moment here. The church reached out and served the community in very meaningful ways that made a difference to peoples' lives. It was not harnessed by the rules and regulations of the institution; rather it bypassed these and expressed its witness in ways that mattered. I did some 'churchy' duties with the Sunday school, the ladies meetings, the fetes, fund raising and attending the most frightful soirees. The soirees were held in the drawing rooms of magnificent houses around Sefton Park. At these events I had to listen to gracious silver haired, kind hearted and sweet natured but ancient ladies with crinkly faces and wobbling chins sing their hearts out with high, reedy voices. They were like Hinge and Bracket, but for real.

I was always given pride of place in the front row at such soirees and concerts. Rarely was I able to sit next to Henry as he was always asked to introduce items or accompany the guests of honour. I was, even though I sat at the front, the 'also ran.' I watched devotedly as past it 'plumpies', dressed in the most garish and inappropriate costumes with make-up to match, sang loudly, danced sheepishly and entertained readily. I learned to smile gracefully and sweetly whilst collapsing uncontrollably inside. My most memorable moment was having a coughing fit in the middle of a rendition of 'Nobody loves a fairy when she's forty.' Two gutsy old ladies, with legs as wrinkly as their faces and who could not remember when they had been forty, performed this rendition. They were gallantly attired in short but voluminous fairy costumes that unfortunately revealed flesh in places I didn't know flesh should exist.

I also learned not to comment on sermons, never to let my views be known in church and to accept criticism of Henry without being able to tell the people dishing it out to get lost. It seemed to be an accepted fact that people could come up to me with a grumble about him in the hope I would either speak to him about it or try and solve the problem for them. Cheek!

Church had been a part of my life since I was a child so I was familiar with all aspects of it. However, it had never occurred to me that it could feel so very different from the other side of the fence. I began to feel that spirituality was more important than organised religion and could offer a depth of understanding of the world and the Creator that woman's meetings and such like can not. It concerned me that the spiritual side of religion played such a tiny role in church life. I began to move away from what might be termed 'institutionalised religion'. I never shared these views in the church as it could have jeopardised things for Henry.

We had wonderful neighbours in Montclair Drive, where we lived. None of them were church members so they had no interest in our jobs, just in us as people and this made such a refreshing change. At one side was a university lecturer and at the other a local head master. We laughed a lot with them. At examination time, the lecturer's lawn was immaculate. He dashed up and down this vast area from early morning with a huge old-fashioned mower that clanked and creaked and drowned his colourful swearing. His annoyance with the students who lazily prepared for exams was worth seeing and ensured he had the neatest lawn in the street.

One morning, from the bathroom window of the house on the other side of us, I heard the headmaster's son screaming at the top of his voice 'We're all doomed, I tell you, we're all doomed,' in a brilliant Scottish accent straight out of Dad's Army. This was due to the fact that his ever-patient mother was making this recalcitrant teenager wash his neck. It was so good to have such ordinary human beings surround us at home.

We had a huge garden at this house and looked after it very efficiently. Our legacy to those who followed was a small but well-formed Cypress tree, planted in the middle of a pretty flowerbed in the centre of the lawn. When we returned many years later it was enormous and the incumbent was cursing the person who had planted such a monstrosity and, I am ashamed to say, we kept quiet.

As a clergy wife you learn very quickly that you cannot have many real friends in the congregation, for if you do others who are not your personal friends will be jealous and it leads to inter congregation warfare of the most unpleasant kind. Therefore life is quite lonely. Clergy wives are very supportive of each other and we had many happy meetings for clergy wives in this city where we could talk without fear of offending someone and gossip happily to our heart's content. Happily, in each of the churches Henry has led we have made a few very good and loyal friends who have kept the friendship discreet and have remained friends through the years.

Having a tall, strong, youngish and handsome husband was somewhat of a disadvantage, but his status did help to keep some of the ladies of the congregation in control. It is amazing the effect that a piece of white plastic cut out from a washing up bottle has when worn around the neck of a person of the male sex. Quite a number of bejewelled and heavily made-up older ladies swooned somewhat at his feet and their eyelashes, weighted down by thick, gooey, 'wet and lick' mascara, stuck together as they tried to flutter them sexily in his direction. They would have probably have passed out had they known what a passionate side he had to him. The number of times I was swooped up into those large arms and devoured was wonderful.

On one occasion when he visited a gracious, charming, sweet and elegant old lady, she stood up to greet him in her superbly appointed flat. As she gathered herself and straightened her back her silk knickers promptly fell to the ground in a wrinkled heap about her ankles. An embarrassed Henry made an excuse to speak to the maid and on his return the offending garment had disappeared. He always said he was dying to know where she had put them.

Another church, that had to be closed down, was attached to Henry's care. It was situated in an extremely poor community and had a few really colourful personalities in it. Let me explain. A couple of old sisters, whose age was impossible to ascertain beneath the layers of clothing, dirt and matted hair surrounding their faces, lived in the basement of a large Victorian terrace near this church. They shared their basement with approx thirty rabbits and forty cats. The flat had earth floors. Can you imagine the smell?

One evening they had a small fire in their flat and the poor firemen had to carry them out to the ambulance that took them to hospital. On arrival at the hospital they were bathed, deloused and provided with clean attire by extremely patient nurses. When Henry visited it was difficult to recognise them in their new, clean state. The nursing staff deserved a medal for their kindness and care. Whilst the ladies were in hospital the RSPCA arrived at their flat and had to journey back and forth all day, catching animals and taking them to be re-homed. The firemen tidied up the house and made it safe and secure. The old ladies, on their return, were furious as they could not find anything. They had not been used to tidiness or cleanliness. It was hard to believe that it was the early 1970's. It felt more like the Victorian era.

These ladies loved coming to church because it was warm, the people were kind, they received regular parcels of food and they were cared for well by the congregation. One Sunday evening they sat in the pews and made an awful commotion. Henry asked if they were okay and one of them said she wanted to go to the toilet. He told her just to go quietly through to the lavatory, but, 'whoops, too late,' she told Henry in a very loud and reedy voice, much to the amusement of the congregation. He discreetly asked if she would like to 'tidy herself up'. 'No, 'it'll dry quickly', she answered. The aroma drifting along the pews was unmentionable.

They were quite wily old characters, as we found out when the police brought them home one afternoon. They had taken themselves to a holiday camp in Wales for their annual two-week holiday and on leaving they were stopped and requested to pay for the holiday. Their answer was that the advert only said to send a small deposit and two weeks holiday was theirs, it didn't mention anything about more money. The staff said they would keep the suitcases as collateral until the ladies could pay. They were very happy for the company to do so. You see, the cases were full of clothes from jumble sales and they knew they could replace everything for pennies. This ruse worked for about three years, believe it or not.

During another service we heard a fumbling at the back of the church and on investigating, found someone was stealing the carpet. On many occasions the communion wine appeared to evaporate. The church officer was an alcoholic and couldn't resist the temptation. As we packed up the furnishings on closing the church, police arrived and asked us to lock the doors because there was a gunfight outside. It was more like the 'OK' Coral than Liverpool.

Henry had much social work to do here. This included taking folk to the social security office to help them complete difficult forms, as many found reading and writing difficult. One day when he entered, a nun from the Catholic Church was also there on a similar errand. A chap entered, took one look at the clergyman and the nun and in a big, gruff, scouse voice, announced "My God, things must be bad if the Pope's laying them off'. The folk here may not have had much in terms of worldly goods but they certainly had a great sense of humour.

I became pregnant and everyone was delighted – it was a big event to have a church baby and this had not happened for many years. You see, when you marry a clergyman you become the property of the church. The expected baby is a 'church baby.' They take surrogate ownership of the pregnancy and the baby.

The ladies of the congregation all thought they knew better than me how I should look after myself and what I should do during pregnancy etc. They knew what I should eat and not eat, how heavy I should be and what I needed to buy. Well, I was the one who had been 'seen to' by their precious clergyman and it was 'my' baby, not theirs. I do remember though, one very kind, bowed lady in her nineties who knitted a pair of bootees for the forthcoming sprog using an old Quaker pattern. She said the baby would never be able to kick them off and she was absolutely right.

Strangely, I remember vividly the months before the birth, the fading sense of freedom as an individual and the last visages of having to think only of ourselves. On a last visit to the hospital before the baby was born, I walked slowly and laboriously to the clinic, carrying this enormous weight in front of me up the hill. The sky was a brilliant blue and the November day was cold, crisp and clear. I felt sad and happy at the same time. Sad because I would never again be totally free and happy because this baby was so wanted.

Nine months had passed quickly. I attended all the requisite natural childbirth classes. The 'in thing' was to have your baby naturally. So I learnt how to breathe, to focus on a calm thought and sing a tune for the painful bits. Henry also learned the tune (it was 10 green bottles) too. I have detested that tune ever since and have never once sung it with my classes in all the years I have taught. A cold shiver of agony travels right along my spine even now if I ever I hear a class singing it.

The problem with the natural childbirth classes was that the staff were not totally honest. They did not actually tell us the whole truth about how bad the painful bits were or how aggressive we could become to those around us. As the end of the pregnancy approached, it was discovered that I could not go into labour on my own, I lacked some particular chemical in my blood and I needed help, so off I trotted to be induced. The words naïve, innocent and slaughter come to mind!

As I entered the large teaching hospital I recalled the very prestigious reputation it had and thought to myself, I am fit and healthy so what can possibly go wrong. Yes, you've guessed, everything. After twenty-four hours of excruciating labour, I went through the indignity of being examined, legs akimbo, by a parade of trainee doctors. In those days your permission for such an exhibition was not requested. I was so past it by then they could have used the images for a porn video for all I had cared. After enduring a ride in a wheelchair to the radiography department and being x-rayed, I was told there was just enough room for the baby to be born naturally. So I was wheeled back again, this time to the labour ward.

I persevered using gas and air, shouting obscenities at Henry and begging for painkillers that never came. I began to wish I had never decided to have a child and all the other chaotic things those women in labour wish. The nurses took it all in their stride. Henry was then sent out of the room as the doctor decided the baby was distressed and the dreaded forceps were brought in. The sight of them helped me give birth. The baby was shown to me for a few seconds and then I was stitched up. After such an experience I would never be shy of any examinations ever again, I was past it. I then fell into a gas-induced slumber. When I awoke a little later I was totally on my own in the room, on the uncomfortable bed, with no baby. I panicked, as I couldn't remember being shown the baby. I shouted for a nurse who told me that the baby had been taken away and placed in an incubator and her chest had been cleaned out to help her breathe properly.

Two hours later Henry caught a nurse to ask what was happening, only to be told our daughter had been born soon after he was sent out. He was allowed to see her with me and she went back into the incubator. This was very unfair to him, it prevented me from establishing an early relationship and bond with my daughter and we never forgave the hospital for the shabby treatment we received.

I learnt how to sit gingerly on an inflatable ring and every time I see a child with one in the swimming pool the memories return. I cried on my husband's shoulders in the hospital because this little scrap in the incubator was so quiet. How naïve of me, I should have been making the most of each silent moment. Apart from feeding and visiting times, the babies had to stay in the nursery. As Henry waited one evening the fathers were looking at the babies in the cots behind the nursery window. He commented on the beautiful black baby in the first cot to which a deep voice replied, 'It's probably mine, the wife burns everything.' All the fathers, including that of the baby in question, simply dissolved into laughter.

Ten days later I proudly took our daughter home and this was a very happy time for us. I had never handled a baby before and was not absolutely sure what to do, but I was a quick learner and she made her needs known very clearly. I did understand folk who felt as if they could shout at babies. Our baby was one of those who, having got home, let it all hang out and cried loudly and incessantly both day and night for no reason at all. But, she was beautiful and a real independent little character. We decided to call her Naomi and she was christened during a normal Sunday service with no fuss, no god parents and no fanfare. It was what we wanted so it was what we did. As you can imagine, every person in the congregation knew better than this young wife how to keep the baby quiet. They offered all kinds of solutions to stop the crying, but few of them offered to have her cry in their house for a few hours to give us a break.

I was slowly beginning to realise that there was a third person in our marriage – the church. She was a relentless mistress, hungry for attention and greedy for time. She never gave up in her demands and ate slowly away at the edges of relationships. She wanted her partner for herself and did not like to share. When a wife wanted her husband's attention, the mistress was there in her many guises to steal him away. Time did not age her or slow down her demands and her expectations grew as the years passed. She could not be shamed into submission, bought off or thrown to one side, she was all consuming. She did not disappear and leave me the man I married until he finally left her clutches a good thirty years hence.

After Naomi's birth my back was very bad, I used to crawl up and down the stairs on my behind because the pain was excruciating and I could not bend at all. A kind and thoughtful church member, who was a consultant orthopaedic surgeon, gave me a corset to wear and told me to be very careful. It was rather like an old-fashioned weapon of torture. Much later in life I was told I should really not have given birth naturally, I should have had a Caesarean. Not much use after the event.

Our daughter was beautiful, with a mass of black hair. Now neither of us have black hair, so what had happened here I wonder? She had a mind of her own, a will of iron and a smile that dissolved all those around her. She was speaking quite fluently by the time she was two but she tended to speak only when she felt to do so was worthwhile. When Naomi was two and a half, I returned to work part-time and I left her father to look after her for a couple of mornings a week until we found a local nursery place for her.

During these mornings I worked in a school for the blind. The children here taught me far more than I could ever teach them, especially about how we sighted people see the world. We only see the world lazily with our eyes. They saw it with their ears, their noses, their hands and if they were lucky, a little part of their eyes. I taught them to play the piano and their skill and feeling was immense. They were incredible fun. They taught me to appreciate what I had, not to want more and to be happy. Many delicate children also attended the school and it was my first introduction to physical special needs. I soon realised that every child is special and every child deserves the best.

Arriving home after lunch one day Naomi looked me straight in the eye and with a very solemn expression on her face told me, 'daddy pushed my food in my face'. This was such a clear and well-constructed sentence for a two year old. She was always difficult at meal times and he had just lost it and pushed the spoon in her mouth. Her articulation shocked him and it never happened again. Of course she wound him around her little fingers as daughters do and, although she may have driven him crazy, as she grew older she could still dissolve him into laughter and get what she wanted with consummate ease.

We became friends with a couple who were doctors and who had two small boys, Callum and Niall. Our children all got on very well together, which was a bonus for us. It was great to chat to another young mother about simple problems that we both experienced. I well remember one Christmas when we gathered the children in our house for a party and Henry dressed up as Father Christmas. He donned the costume in a neighbour's house and came striding up the street ringing a loud bell. The children were between three and five years so they were consumed with excitement. The charade passed off beautifully. None of them recognised him, not even the astute Naomi. The time came for him to go back to his reindeer. As he left the house in the approaching darkness, the children insisted they went to the gate to wave him goodbye. He trotted a few steps and looked back – they were still there. He had to walk to the bottom of the road and around the corner before they would come into the house. I cannot repeat in print his description of how silly he felt, however it was worth it to see the magic on their faces. When he returned Naomi gave him such a telling off for missing Father Christmas!

During this time the gremlin (mother-in-law) was always lurking in the background. Every time we went to Newcastle she demanded an audience, especially if she thought we would be visiting my parents. She played each of her children against the other. She talked about how wonderful or successful the other children and grandchildren were, not showing an iota of interest in those visiting her. It was not until years later that each brother and sister realised the intrigue and power she wielded by doing this. Many is the time I have regretted giving in to this tirade and missing the opportunity to be with my parents, who were so good to us.

At this time, my parents decided we had a precarious lifestyle. We lived in a 'tithed' house and anyone who has experienced this will know what I mean. Actually in the ministry the house is supposed to be a part of the salary but this never seems to be understood by anyone. The church is the landlord and more often than not, they are not effective landlords. Clergy are always expected to be grateful for the smallest nail given to them. We had to beg to have the toilet repaired. We were regarded as ungrateful if we commented that we were living in a kitchen that was modern 100 years ago. When it comes to decorating, well, the house is usually redecorated before your arrival and after that you are generally on your own chum.

So my parents bought a cottage in Anglesey for the benefit of the children and us. This was their way of making sure of provision for the children mainly, but of course also for us if anything went wrong. The cottage was inexpensive to purchase because it needed an awful lot of work, so part of the bargain was that we would do the work. Now, when your husband's salary is just outside the limit for claiming state benefits it is not easy finding money for new roofs etc. Somehow we did it. He played drums as much as he could and I did a lot of supply teaching.

The church house in Montclair Drive began to have a very distinctive smell about it. When Henry mentioned this to the church elders, the 'man who knew everything', was despatched by them to discover what it was. Now all within the church circles revered this man. His formal title was the 'Chairman of the Fabric Committee'. In other words, he was a very powerful figure who commanded ultimate allegiance. He was the DIY man of unending knowledge at the church. We called him the 'destroy it thyself wallah.' There was nothing about buildings, whether they were churches or houses that he did not know. In fact he was the original 'Mr Fix It'. He could mend and decorate everything with his bags of old nails and screws collected over the previous century, and his pots of paint left over from various jobs here and there. The truth of the matter was that little he did worked, so eventually we got an expert in ourselves and found we had dry rot.

When the workmen came to take the plaster from the walls our daughter was allergic to the plaster dust and developed an awful form of impetigo. The church elders were horrified and kindly moved us into a hotel. It was lovely to be looked after. However every time I went to breakfast I felt violently sick and had to return to my room. I found out I was pregnant again. This time, I was to experience the dreaded morning sickness. It was so annoying not to be able to appreciate the sumptuous breakfasts and the careful service.

I kept teaching and one day I nursed a blind pupil who was very tearful. Later that week the headmaster rang in a complete state of panic to tell me the child had German measles. I was of the generation before vaccination. It was a stomach churning moment when I understood the expression about blood running cold. What could we do? I visited the doctor who passed the problem straight back to me and said we had to consider what we wanted to do. We made the decision to carry on and forget about it, as we would love the baby whatever happened, but every day of the pregnancy I was niggled by worries of possible problems.

My heightened perception or 'second sight' came in quite useful when we lived in this area. Henry was asked to conduct an exorcism in a house where the family, especially the children, were plagued by poltergeists. The children were almost at the point of refusing to enter because objects were hurled at them. He asked me to go to the house with him to meet the family. It was a perfectly ordinary house but to me it felt very cold inside. I felt distinctly uncomfortable and could not wait to get out. Following the exorcism service I returned and the whole atmosphere had altered, it had returned to the feel of a happy family house and the children were racing around happily inside.

Henry has often been unnerved by my particularly accurate perception of a person after just a passing meeting, and it is something I cannot explain. What is even worse is when, so often, I can relate what he has been thinking, or tell exactly when my children will phone me. I have never exploited this sense or explored it further as it was not something that the church would have considered acceptable. Only once did this sense let me down and I will come to that later.

CHAPTER 4

Down South

I suppose this is where the fun really starts. It was 1975, the age of 'Superwoman'. She was everywhere, in magazines, on the television, in your face. In fact a book was written on how to become a superwoman. It was a suitable thickness to stop doors banging shut in the wind. I hated that woman with a real passion. Not only could she do anything and everything, she did them exceptionally well and still managed to look calm and collected. I never really believed in her. I knew the reason she never had a child's food down her clothes, was never 'peed' on when changing nappies, never had to lie on the bed to get the zip on the tight jeans to close and always had beautifully coiffured hair was because of the army of nannies, helps and hairdressers hidden behind the cameras.

As the wife of a clergyman I had to be prepared to give up home, leave friends behind and move house when either the church or, as the purists like to believe, ' the spirit', guided Henry. Well, 'the spirit' moved him to take charge of a new and exciting ecumenical experiment, a 'church without walls', in Hemel Hempstead. I was expected to be Superwoman, to organise the move, to pack up, to look after our daughter, to continue teaching, be sick when I had a spare moment and forget about being pregnant. It didn't work, but eventually we were ready to roll south. The furniture van took us to a new, unfinished housing estate, Woodhall Farm, on the outskirts of the town.

This was a country area with plenty of open space, fields, and trees. Our children loved it and it certainly was great for kids. I got plenty of exercise as the nearest shops were over a mile each way. There was no church on this estate or any other public services. It was quite a few years before shops, schools, buses and medical facilities appeared. We were given a brand new detached house on a large corner plot, a situation virtually unheard of in church circles, and it was comfortable. It was wonderful to feel like ordinary folk. There were so few houses when we first moved there that one morning, when we opened the front door, a horse stuck his head through and neighed loudly at us. After all, this had been his territory and here we were building our own stable there!

The summer of 1975 when we moved was hot with weeks of unending sunshine and no rain. We awoke to vivid blue skies that stayed like that all day long. Our house had the typical new house garden, one inch of soil and six inches of builder's rubble. We got to work to turn it into something that resembled a shape. In fact, whilst trying to help dig the garden I ended up with a broken wrist because the rubble below was so thick and hard. It was only a minor break though and not enough to warrant stopping doing any of the things expected of me.

Henry battled gamely against the rubble to lay a crazy paved patio for us. It was very helpful that he was tall and strong and could wield a pickaxe manfully. He lost an enormous amount of weight in the heat as he worked. It was a real bonus having this patio at the back of the house where no one could see us and we could be ourselves. Some of the days were so hot we could drop an egg on the concrete and it would cook. As I grew bigger and bigger the heat was uncomfortable and this baby seemed to be enormous all around, I was beginning to look like Tweedle Dee.

We planted a long fence of blackberries that in future years were to overtake us and provide pounds and pounds of fruit each summer that we turned into jam. We accepted gifts of apples from friends and turned them into chutney that saw us through the winter. I loved and still love cooking so it was a pleasure to bake everything and it also saved money. My only problem that was my baking sometimes did not even reach the oven as Henry stole the dough and the mixes from the bowl if I was looking the other way.

Our son, Christopher, was born in the December of 1975. He was a great baby, good natured and content. He was born in a small local hospital at the time of the doctor's strike. He had to be induced and I was dreading the experience, but I need not have worried. It was a lovely birth. This time Henry was with me throughout and he was ecstatic to see his son born. I held the baby immediately and recovered very quickly. In fact, so quickly they said I could go home earlier than expected. Naomi explained to me that Henry was like a whirling dervish trying to get the house tidy. She was very good at telling tales.

I forgot to mention, you see, that I was chief cook, bottle washer, cleaner and everything else. This is what I believe is now referred to as 'multi-tasking' and it seems some writers think it a new phenomenon. Well, I have to inform them that it has been a fact of female life since time began. Henry always said that when he tried to help it was 'never good enough'. When chatting with friends and neighbours it appeared that every other male in the neighbourhood said the same thing – I think it must be an inherent feature of the male psyche!

I am sure that any men reading will fully understand this and no doubt feel they have also suffered in the same way. I also have no doubt that many females reading this will be smiling quietly with a knowing look on their faces, thinking, yes, been there, done that, got the tee-shirt. Will there ever be understanding between the sexes over housework? I rather think not.

We had so little money in this parish we had the first pickings from church jumble sales. I would buy large dresses with lots of material and then cut them up to make dresses for Naomi. My best result was a camel coat I made her from a voluminous adult coat I bought for 25pence. My friends were very kind and passed on their children's clothes when they were outgrown. My parents really clothed both children for us. My biggest disaster was a sweater I knitted for Henry with wool I had bought for 30p. As I worked, this garment became heavier and heavier. I thought this was just because he was over six feet tall and, with me being only five feet tall, any item would appear large. When I finished and stitched it together we were paralytic with laughter. The sleeves reached the floor and the sweater was almost down to his knees. He was such a great person though he volunteered to wear it just because I had made it for him. I was not so great and could not bear the embarrassment amongst friends and colleagues when they saw the monstrosity, so it disappeared quietly.

After that knitting was out, much to the criticism of the gremlin. She of course was a wonderful knitter and this only served to rub salt in my wounds. However, although she was so good, she never managed to knit for our children or us. I stuck to sewing of all kinds after that as I found this easier. I designed fabric collages, stitched them, then sold them and did quite well. This money went into the same pot as the drumming – the survival pot.

I had to go back to work to help out again and so began teaching music part-time at a local infant school in the neighbouring estate at Grovehill and Henry looked after the children. I cycled there and back and this kept the figure in trim. The nearest shops were over a mile away so a parade of prams and pushchairs could be seen ploughing their way to and fro each day. This all helped with the fitness campaign, we did not need to go to the gym. We enrolled Naomi at school and I have to say she was not happy. She was bright, inquisitive and an eager learner and had to wait for the others to catch up. She read fluently but the school taught the initial teaching alphabet, an experiment in Hertfordshire at the time. When forced to learn this, Naomi calmly told the teacher, 'my mummy taught me to read and I can read properly.' Not a very diplomatic answer, but Naomi has been honest all her life, although now and again it would help to balance the honesty with a little diplomacy. So we became 'awkward' parents, which was slightly embarrassing since I taught in a school quite near to Naomi's. It certainly brought home to me that bright children need to be stretched to keep them motivated; they do not need more of the same but challenges that stretch them. We just removed her quietly from the school and then told them what we thought of them.

Again we were fortunate to have smashing neighbours who became lifelong friends. They too had small children so all played together happily, joyfully and safely. I expect others may have, like me, found that the time of life when children are young is a very happy and sociable time. We made more friends than at any other time. We all shared the same problems and lived through the same illnesses; had the same troubles, shared lifts to all kinds of activities and gossiped together as we waited for the children to finish their various judo or ballet or riding classes etc. The friends we made at this time are what I call 'golden' friends. They increase in value as the years pass.

We had lots of fun here, noisy summer barbecues, clear blue skies and regular trips to London. On one occasion, Henry had to rush a good friend to hospital in time to give birth. His careful but very fast driving down the motorway saved the day and she arrived in time. This 'baby in a rush' is now a successful police sergeant. But how can this have happened, because it only seems like yesterday that she couldn't wait to get into the world? Although we were in the Home Counties we did experience some hard winters and on one occasion the snow was a foot deep. Opposite our house at that time was a huge mound of earth that was covered in snow and our children went with their friends to sledge down the hill. They returned shortly afterwards informing us that they were not allowed to play. When my neighbour, Jane, and I went outside we found out why. Their fathers were sledging up and down the hill having a great time. We retrieved the sledges and the kids' fun continued.

Henry adored the children and was excellent with them, apart from the feeding incident with Naomi. He made her a gorgeous dolls house and a ride on tractor for Christopher. His talents as a draughtsman and engineer were put to good effect as he designed and then built the toys. Had he the time he could quite easily have made all kinds of toys, but the church is an unrelenting taskmaster and gobbles time as no other job.

This new estate, as was the situation with many others in the countryside around London, was a growing area populated by upwardly mobile families. Young fathers on the way to success and higher management were moving to the estate to buy bigger homes and show everyone how well they were doing. They were also very keen to have better furniture, bigger cars, more innovative garden designs and everything better than their neighbour. It was also the time when 'wife swapping' became popular in certain circles. Some houses on the estate were the sort of place where, if you dropped your keys, this was taken as indication of what you were 'up for.' We knew all about what was happening and who was involved, as we tended to pick up the pieces when the partners came to us to talk about the pain and hurt they were suffering after such parties.

This was a place of considerable tension as well as much fun and happiness. Many couples were trying to climb rickety and unstable ladders that were perched against the unsteady walls of firms being set up quickly and dissolved just as quickly. Individuals wanted to have their cakes, eat them and then ask for more. The problem was that they could not deal with the indigestion that followed. Always the cake had to be newer, more luxurious and more sought after than their friends.

One neighbour, always generous with company, simply had to be the first to have every new thing and when the tension spilled over into having new mates, the marriage dissolved and finally suicide overcame him. What a terribly sad end for a lovely person who was simply eaten up and spat out by a greedy world.

Plenty of the housewives who were stuck out on a lonely estate thought an attractive clergyman fair game. They made themselves look very attractive and then visited us to ask if he could help them with a problem. In truth, they were the problem. We had a middle-aged lady who spread the rumour that Henry could not keep away from her house. The expression he used when describing her suggested otherwise however. Many ladies wanted to be more glamorous, better and bigger than everyone else, and this included their figures. Some had 'boob jobs' and unnecessary tucks and lifts to help them achieve the 'look' they so coveted. They flashed their unmoving footballs around before us all as they paraded through the estate, teetering in their Italian shoes and designer clothes. We all commented on how good they looked. However we were typical gossipy and catty females below the surface and quite a few less than complementary comments passed between us when out of their earshot. I really cannot understand how women who do not need surgery choose to be cut up and stitched and face possible infections for vanity.

Many who had the surgery still did not love themselves afterwards, so the money was really wasted. Sadly women are often never satisfied with what they have and always yearn for something different. If hair is naturally blonde, as mine was, we dye it dark, as I did. If it is dark, we dye it blonde. When we are thin we try all possible methods to gain weight and if we are fat, we spend a fortune trying to get thin. If more of us could celebrate ourselves as we are, I am sure there would be far more happy people in the world.

Plenty of people around the area where we lived needed help. Some found it hard to live in the country away from shops and friends. In such an environment, when you are on the up then everything is rosy. When you are on the way down, the hill is steep, the fall quick and the bottom hard and stony. Many fell by the wayside and often came to us for all kinds of help. Many times we found ourselves helping others out financially, with food, with assistance in claiming benefits, or simply supporting. Listening to problems took up a major chunk of time. We heard about relationships breaking up, partnerships riddled with mistrust and catalogues of lies that resulted in huge debts within marriages. It seemed that those who suffered most were those trying to come to terms with lies and deceit in their relationship. The lies were rather like computer worms, infiltrating all layers of life. They infected truth and were very difficult to eradicate. A partner often felt that if the 'other half' could blithely tell one lie, then what else in the relationship could be believed? Some folk learned to live with the damage; others felt they wanted to find a new partner who was 'worm free'.

Whether those around us were church orientated or not mattered not one jot if they were in trouble. They expected us to help and be available. You see, the general public visualised the clergy house as being a place of love and charity. Our children were expected to share their toys and their parents and be true Christian children. Why, I asked myself? The children gradually became angry at such expectations and resented people coming and infiltrating their personal territory. These reactions were perfectly normal and to be expected in such a situation.

The success of the whole project resulted in us outgrowing our accommodation. Consequently, it was decided the house had to be enlarged. This was great because it provided a private area for the family and we could all have our own personal space. We moved out whilst the alterations were completed, but no chance of hotel accommodation here, as had been the case in our previous church. A sweet elderly couple at the far side of the town accommodated us. They were exceptionally kind and caring people, but imagine decamping a young family and parents into one bedroom in a house full of treasures. Rather a difficult experience, but of course we kept smiling as this was expected of us.

The ecumenical experiment continued to be a roaring success. Henry participated in many activities and services in other denominations. The sharing and understanding of work and service between denominations produced a vibrant community of Christian people who worked out their witness in ways appropriate to each, without the chains of institutionalised religion. It became quite clear to me that going to a church building on a Sunday does not make a person a Christian any more than standing in a garage makes a person a car. The usual requests for hatch, match and dispatch services continued and I well remember one funeral when Henry had an unforgettable experience. Gravediggers usually leave a little box of earth adjacent to the grave to be used when the words 'earth to earth' are said. Henry leaned over and picked up the material and threw it into the grave. He thought it made an odd sound so while he led the prayer and folk bowed their heads, he looked down. Lo and behold, a spent tea-bag was lying on top of the coffin. He had picked up the remains of the gravediggers tea!!

Occasionally Henry took part in formal Church occasions. For example, he was a member of the congregation at Canterbury when the Pope came and this was a memorable event indeed. He also shared in confirmation services at St Alban's Abbey when folks from the estate wished to be confirmed into the Anglican faith. These were ornate, stately and dignified services. I took our young, four year old daughter to watch, and managed to get a seat next to the aisle so she could see her father in the procession. As the Bishop and his entourage processed up the Abbey in all their finery, I held Naomi up to watch. In her piercing and reedy little voice, she proclaimed loudly with mounting excitement, 'mummy, the clowns are coming, the clowns are coming.' Needless to say those around just dissolved into laughter, which somewhat detracted from the solemnity of the occasion, but I expect those hallowed walls have heard worse throughout the ages.

When Cardinal Hume visited the ecumenical church on the neighbouring estate we attended the service and I will never forget his sense of presence and how he spent time with everyone. Christopher was only five and had taken an 'Action man' toy to play with. At the end of the service the Cardinal saw this and stopped to talk him. He had a long conversation about the toy and it was as if no one else existed except him and Christopher. He told us that he regretted not being able to have children. His calmness and serenity left a lasting effect upon us.

Whilst we lived here my grandmother died and left me all her lovely jewellery. Of course we stored it away safely but we were burgled twice. The first time all the jewellery, including some really beautiful antiques, was taken. The police said it would have been sold immediately so there was no chance of retrieving it. Nor could it be replaced because it was antique. The second time the burglars broke everything in the house, including the beautiful china we had received as wedding presents and the children's toys. They also took all my husbands clothes. Clearly they had no taste. The burglar was caught and jailed but nothing returned.

The police said we should get a dog. So we got a dog, a Doberman. This was our first dog and what a breed to choose. She was rather like our daughter, independent minded, strong willed and demanding. That is probably why the two were so good with each other. Have you ever tried to train a Doberman? Our legs got shorter by the day and the dog became fitter because we walked so much.

One night she raised hell and we ignored her – the next morning we found someone had stolen our trailer from the drive. Poor dog, she had tried. We were never burgled again as soon as everyone knew about the dog. She looked fierce but was a real softie. The children dressed her up and played happy families with her and she loved it. She would let anyone into the house but would only let them out if we gave permission. We sold some chairs we did not need and as the lady buying them came to leave the dog stood in front of her and growled menacingly. She could only leave when we gave her permission, in sight of the dog.

Because of the type of ministry this was, Henry was on duty all the hours of the day and night. How many normal families, I wonder, have meals interrupted regularly for a husband to leave the table, put his meal in the hotplate and go to console an unhappy wife or a distressed father? How many wives have had their husband leave in the middle of a family celebration to go and help someone at the end of his or her tether? This was a regular occurrence we learned to live with.

My children grew up knowing they were watched. Their friends could be absolute horrors, run around with snotty noses, with guns as toys, in states of constant dishevelment and no one batted an eyelid. However, if either of our children acted out of turn the whole estate knew about it because, of course, they were the clergy children. My daughter is a shrewd and calculating girl and grew up able to handle such attitudes. She learned how to stop anyone criticising her from 100 paces with either a withering look or a cutting phrase. Christopher was not so lucky, he hurt easily, so he had to be watched and supported more closely.

During our time here I caught pneumonia and was signed off work for five months. I could not recall ever having been so tired in my life. I couldn't get out of bed without help. I collapsed when going to the toilet one night and remember staying on the floor until my husband found me in the morning. I was too weak to shout for help. Henry looked after me very well and my parents came when they could. His one mistake was, when I began to feel better, to cook me a special meal. It was a huge plate of liver and onions. Now bearing in mind he couldn't cook, this was a major success and a real meal of love but not exactly appetising to an invalid. How I ate it I shall never know. Naomi was a natural organiser, she took control of the kitchen and the cleaning and organised her father and brother exceptionally well.

Apart from this illness, we had a freedom of mind and spirit in this parish that we had never experienced before or since, because there was no huge church building to bow down to, to heat and light, to find funds to keep going when it was only really used for marriages and funerals and no wretched committees to keep happy. It gave Henry the opportunity to witness as he wished, to share thoughts without restrictions and to help people as he felt the spirit moved.

One advantage of being a teacher is that you have the same holidays as your children. This does not mean to say that you are any more efficient at amusing them than the next parents. I admit I always found it hard work finding things to keep children happy for six weeks and it helped me understand that holidays can be a nightmare for parents who are suddenly confronted with a child for company day in and day out without a break. I found the children and I needed space during the day, for different reasons, so we had an agreed 'personal space' time. I encouraged them to read a book, play in the garden or do a crossword while I had a coffee, read the newspaper, put my feet up or just chilled out for an hour.

I tried to gather together a variety of things to do during the holidays, some noisy, some active, some quiet. I asked the local sports centre and library what courses were available, what was free, when children's swimming times and sports clubs were etc. It made a huge difference having all this information before the holidays began. I knew that, when the holiday ended, the children would have to get back into the school routine so I tried to keep some parts of the routine going. For example, I made sure they were both washed and dressed before they came for breakfast and that they put their clothes in a neat pile in their bedroom before they went to bed. Don't laugh; it really was not as hard as it sounds, though sometimes I do admit I lost the motivation to stick to it. Holiday bedtimes were a little later than usual but as the holiday came to an end, I made sure bedtimes were back to normal, so that when school started the children were back into the routine of earlier bed-times.

Many activities needed little finance but were great fun. My children loved putting mustard and cress seeds on wet cotton wool in empty plastic margarine tubs and watering them daily, measuring their growth and finally cutting them and making sandwiches to eat.

I was never very good at persuading them to help me with the housework. They obviously took after their dad there. All children love to bake, if you can stand the mess. As a teacher, I knew it was important to let them make a mess but as a housewife it still drove me mad seeing the kitchen look like an explosion had taken place. I put newspapers on the floor under the table and this helped me to clear up the mess more quickly. Making salt dough was great as it could be used again and again to make and bake models. My friend had me in stitches as she made cakes using salt dough and then tried to eat them, not realising it was for play only.

I always hoarded old catalogues for cutting up and making pictures from and I would scrounge an old roll of wallpaper from someone as the plain back of it made a great frieze. The children drew a different picture each day and made up a story to go with it and it kept them occupied for ages. Before the holidays began I collected outrageous party frocks, hats and jewellery and put them in a dressing up box. All their friends loved dressing up and played happily for a long time.

The one thing I did like about holidays was the time I could spend listening to the children. They had such a simple, clear and very perceptive view of the world, uncluttered by experience. They would tell me about their day before they went to sleep each night and we always got them to read before they went to sleep. Books were expensive so we bought them at jumble sales and joined the local library.

On occasion I found that some of Naomi and Christopher's friends would get very worried before the holidays as they were to be shared between two parents who clearly did not get on with each other. It was and still is so important for separated couples not to deride each other in front of the children. It is not the child's fault that a marriage fails so parents must not use them as weapons. The parents who really loved their children tried to accommodate each other when discussing access. I found those who kept relationships cordial helped the children develop emotionally into much stronger people with fewer hang-ups.

CHAPTER 5
Reality Check Ahead

You know, life is a funny thing. When you think things might just be going well it comes back and kicks you again, and again, and again.

I had started a playgroup in our house when the church extended the house and it was always full. At this time a lady who was 'sort of' interested in the church project attached herself to us, but mostly to Henry. He was still dark, charismatic and charming as well as wearing a dog collar, which seemed to attract both sexes of all ages. She was the type of woman who talked vociferously and animatedly when he was with me but would ignore me when he was not there. I have to admit I did not like her but I just ignored the situation. How wrong I was.

When I was at work she would come to help with church groups, then stay to tidy up and chat to Henry. She didn't need to work so had lots of spare time and gave him a listening ear, pandered to his needs, stroked and flattered his ego. He regarded this as a platonic friendship and liked the attention she paid him. She had other ideas. This was partly my fault, because I was racing around trying to work, keep the house and look after the children so I had no time to listen to a husband.

My neighbours were far more observant than me and watched the situation for some time. They were upset at how openly this woman arrived at the house when I had departed and how friendly she was to Henry. They watched her sidle into Henry's life more and more and show how she enjoyed his friendship and companionship when I was not there. Henry only ever sees the best in people; he often cannot read the subtle signals that females in particular provide. In this respect he is very naïve, or he is a bloody good actor. I prefer to believe he is naïve. My good friends gently opened my eyes as to what was happening. They were amazing and remained supportive of us both. From what I was told, they gave the lady in question a very cold shoulder and isolated her from conversations and meetings. Good!

The problem is, you see, a clergy wife is supposed to be all sweetness and light, never have any troubles, is loyal and faithful and works her fingers to the bone for the church. This of course is utter balderdash. A clergy wife is the same as any other wife and feels the same pain and searing hurt as any other wife in this position. This episode upset me terribly, partly because I knew my inattention had been a contributing factor. I was astonished to know that my close friends had seen what was going on but were undecided for a long while as to whether or not to say anything. That is when I realised that you yourself are always the last to see. This is, though, something that a clergy wife just has to get used to. Mostly it is possible to spot the 'hangers on' a mile away. They smile at him widely whilst totally ignoring you. They drool over him, hang on to his every word, and make a point of being wherever he is. They love the kudos that goes with the job and if they can, they will try to love the incumbent too. The discerning wife can usually dispose of the groupie pretty fast by being 'extra friendly' and saying a few 'choice words' in a few choice places. Sadly, if, like me, you were working all hours of the day, you could sometimes miss this and end up in my situation.

At this time, many of my friends were suffering in their own lives. Their husbands were working longer hours to become high-fliers, giving in to temptations and thus causing the inevitable pain such encounters brought. However, because they owned their houses and their husbands earned good salaries they had enough capital, if they needed it, to have a break or leave and survive comfortably. We were all encouraged by Gloria Gaynor's version of 'I will survive.' It spoke to us and was sung with such gusto it almost burst the lungs.

At this time, Henry lost a lot of his close family, especially the male members, and it had devastating consequences. His grief mounted and, together with his tiredness from an unceasingly heavy workload, contributed to a breakdown through which he tried to keep working. This was a time of hell for both of us. All his male role models were gone and I was on the receiving end of his anger, aggression and hate. I had very good, loyal friends who supported me superbly. Henry went for expert counselling and this helped a lot. Slowly he gained strength and regained his health. For the family, it became a question of reacting to situations as they occurred. The counselling was very painful for him and brought many demons to the fore. I admired him for sticking with it because it was not easy. Throughout, he kept his job going and I supported in whatever way I could.

At his worst he accused me of everything he hated in his mother and shouted at me as if I were she; however we plodded on because actually it was not me who was the problem. To this day he cannot remember what he said or did. If you have ever supported anyone in this condition you will know that you live each day as it happens. You get up in the morning simply hoping that the day will not be too bad and that you will reach evening in one piece. It is agony watching someone that you love go through hell when you are helpless to do anything about it.

All in all, however, I made many very wonderful, long lasting and loyal friends in this place. They are my closest friends to this day who I would trust with my deepest secrets. Friends are the mainstay of life.

As our children grew we had great fun taking them to London every Sunday afternoon, working our way around the museums and sights. Now they have grown up they are adamant that they will take their own children around these museums so we must have got something right. Christmas was very special; we would go into London at dusk and head for Hamley's toy store. We worked our way through each floor, playing with the toys, being told which ones the children would like in their Christmas stockings. Then we would watch the workers scuttling home like little mice, and, when the streets cleared, we would gaze at the sparkling lights.

It was a treat to look in Selfridges's windows and watch the moving displays. Always, there were rows of magical faces at each window engrossed in the fairyland beyond. We would end the night with something to eat and some hot chestnuts from the man cooking them in his brazier on the street corner on the way back to the car. These sound like all the normal things that many other normal happy people did and for us it was a treat to be normal.

I found great happiness in my job. I began to work full-time again and was very fortunate to be able to take Christopher with me and he loved school. He was so good; he never called me mummy at school and acknowledged the difference between me as his mummy and me as a teacher. I still enjoyed teaching and I loved being with children as they are such great fun and so honest, especially the youngest children. If you look a mess they tell you. They notice if you have painted your nails, they comment on your shoes during story time, they share their joys unconditionally with you. It is wonderful when you see on their face that they have understood something. What a privilege it is to help them move on in the world.

It is never easy for teachers who have young families when they are working full time. I found I had to juggle work and family, make decisions as to when to mark books, mount children's work and plan lessons. I made the choice to leave school early and did most of this at home each night when the children went to bed, so that I had some family time with them.

I used the holidays to plan lessons and displays for the forthcoming term. If I wanted children's work to display, I would copy it rather than spend unnecessary time having them copy it out. This was the age of the Banda, a hideous machine that printed work sheets for the teacher. It also left you and your clothes varying shades of purple as the ink ran and smudged everything in sight. How I remember colleagues with purple hands.

Henry was, thank goodness, used to teachers and their foibles. His sisters Roberta and Dorothy and his father were teachers. He knew that the first half hour after arriving home is a dangerous time for teachers when all sorts of stress can be vented on those around, so he trained the children to give me half an hour's space as I came through the door every night. This gave me the time to re-focus from school to family until after the children's bedtime and was a great idea. If ever I forgot I was at home and slipped into teacher mode he would simply say 'Can't get in the kitchen for chalk dust' and I slipped back to mum and wife again.

I was fortunate to be teaching in a lovely primary school in St. Alban's. However, it was the one time in my life when I was embarrassed at school as the head, if I say so myself quite fancied me. My colleagues teased me mercilessly about it. I worked hard at keeping a low profile. We went on a charity walk and he took my picture and kept it. Now this was out of order for a straight-laced girl like me – nice though. Then at a Christmas pantomime when I was dressed up in tights he commented on my legs. I answered by plastering him with a huge custard pie and his fascination for me departed. So did I, and found another job as a deputy-head in another school. I have sympathised with deputies everywhere ever since. This is because as a deputy you are neither 'fish nor fowl.' No longer can you be included in the staff room intrigue because you have a direct line to the boss. The usual staff room gossip about who Mrs so and so was seen with in the town last night is toned down when you are in earshot. I quickly learnt there were disadvantages as well as advantages to having a foot in 'management' especially when management was regarded as 'the other side'.

I was deputy to a very grand lady head. One of the 'old school' who believed everyone should be gracious to her. She was an extremely fashionable and very elegant lady. She was tall, lean and her beautiful white chignon was always immaculate. It is an interesting fact that many of the female heads I worked for had white hair – could this be a free gift with the job I wonder? She had established an excellent school and was benefiting from her hard labours. Her morning was spent reading the newspaper and dealing with the post. The afternoon was spent listening to individual children read to ensure staff were working hard and to make sure children achieved high standards. Everyone was well organised, discipline was superb and the school was highly praised by everyone.

An effective system alerted staff to important visitors. Should such a person arrive a child was sent into each room carrying a pot plant. The child said nothing, just walked through the room. One afternoon, the child duly appeared and staff were just a little more vigilant and cautious, knowing someone was on the premises. The visitor spotted the child and asked whom the plant was for. The child duly told him it was to let the teacher's know someone important was there. The HMI was duly amused and pleased to know he was held in such esteem.

As a deputy it was very good training here for me, because I was given lots of tasks that prepared me extremely well for headship. I was very fond of my boss for, behind all her airs and graces, she really cared about the children and she also cared for her staff, she just didn't want them to know in case they thought she was weak.

The one thing we all detested about her, however, was her little dog that sat in all his glory on the comfy chair in her study. When staff requested an audience we had to stand, so the pooch could sit. He was such a bad-tempered bugger. He would growl under his breath at everyone who entered her study and snap at our ankles as we passed. Many a time I saw a teacher perform a surreptitious kicking technique aimed at his backside, in order to avoid his jaws!

At home, life settled down again as Henry regained his health and momentum and we had all the childhood traumas that all mothers will have been through. The usual ailments plagued our family as all others – we were not immune and we worked our way through chicken pox, mumps and whooping cough. Because

Henry had experienced a fit as a child the medical profession would not vaccinate the children against whooping cough so they had to suffer the illness, which is very debilitating. Experiencing these things kept us on a level with others in the community and we had an immediate point of contact as many other children suffered the same way.

In the 1970's it was much safer for children to play outside during the holidays than it is now and we encouraged this as long as we knew exactly where they were, whom they were with and what time they would return. They knew a minute over time meant we would be out there looking for them and they would be grounded.

Our son split his chin open when his cousin Richard and sister Naomi sent him flying over a seesaw. A good friend, Ray, rushed me to hospital with him so the gaping hole could be stitched. As this little boy lay on the trolley, I stood at the end making soothing noises. I moved forward to hold Christopher's hand and had a full view of the split, which went from one side of his chin to the other and was gaping open for the world to investigate what was inside. The next thing I knew, Ray was sitting me down to recover. Henry was out 'gigging' of course so I had to deal with it on my own.

It is usually such small incidents that cause the most chaos. Naomi tripped over a stone when she was roller-skating and broke her leg. It was as simple as that. When I got her to casualty at West Herts Hospital an old Polish masochist was on duty purporting to be a doctor. He moved her leg around recklessly to ask if it hurt and she squealed like a frightened animal. Have you ever had to listen to such a noise from your child's mouth? It eats through you as nothing else can and you become as defensive as a lion toward your young. Well, I marched into the consultation room and told that doctor exactly what I thought of him and he never laid another finger on her. Another doctor came and suggested her leg was plastered so this was duly done. The masochist left the hospital shortly afterwards and we had free treatment at Harley Street to sort out her leg. Henry was again out gigging. His drumming continued to help us out financially and certainly provided treats for the children.

This parish was experimental and apart from a basic stipend, there were absolutely no extra payments. It was an expensive place to live; we had to provide our own car and do without the niceties usually offered by the parish, so the extra finance from the drumming was very welcome. Being an honest man, Henry declared his drumming income. This was just as well because not everyone likes the clergy and someone living on the estate reported him to the tax office for having a second job. Of course when the men from the Revenue checked they found there was no problem, all was in order. However, his being absent every Friday, Saturday and Sunday night led to quite a lonely existence for me as I sat in and watched other couples having a good time.

We had many different experiences in the area. Probably the most interesting involved a very quiet and personable young man turning up at a worship group one Sunday morning. These groups were held in the extension to the house. He was a kind, gentle and friendly person but said very little about himself. He lived on his own further into the estate. Over time I gained a little more information about him. He told me that he had lived in Russia and his sister was still there. His name was Fergus Maclean. Of course, I put two and two together and he was, in fact, the son of the infamous spy. Although this was fascinating it was Fergus we knew and not his father so he received the same welcome as any other would in our midst. We did have a visit from what I can only describe as' representatives' of the intelligence services. Fergus was clearly being observed and checked out. Thankfully we were found to be plain, genuine, boring folk who were exactly what we purported to be, but it added a little spice to life.

On another occasion, when the miners strike was at its peak Henry wrote a letter of support to the local newspaper and was vociferous in his views. He had been raised in an area of the country where mining was the main industry so he knew how hard the miners worked and how vital the jobs were to their communities. We began to realise that when we made a phone call the phone was not connected immediately and we realised that it was being tapped. We assumed it was because of his vociferous support for the miners. Fancy, such excitement for us ordinary people.

Our car, an orange, automatic Ford estate was a swine. It had a mind of its own and persistently rebelled on us. We could not afford garage fees for repairs so my husband could often be seen, or should I say, heard, trying to mend it. On these occasions it was the language of the shipyards, his previous existence, and not that of the church that could be heard floating through the air. Repairing the car was an occasion when his short temper was at its height. The children and I simply left him to it. We often left the car unlocked in car parks and on town streets in the hope that someone would steal it, but even thieves turned their noses up at it.

After a good few years I obtained a position as head mistress of a tough infant's school in Luton in 1983. I thoroughly enjoyed the job. Now I was a head we could afford a second car and I chose a Morris Minor. I loved my Morris. It was easy to drive, reliable and bumbled along beautifully.

I had many wonderful experiences in this city centre school with a multi-ethnic population. It was such a happy place with wonderful children and parents. The strange thing about being a head is that everyone comes to you to solve his or her problems. On my first morning in this school the secretary showed a parent in to me who had a concern about a teacher. I listened politely and kept thinking to myself – why come to me, go and see the head. Of course it dawned on me that I was the head. Nothing quite prepares you for this moment of destiny!

Almost all head teachers have been classroom teachers at some stage. They know what happens in the classroom and understand the problems that can arise, and so they are usually very supportive of their staff. However, hardly any classroom teachers have been head teachers; so they just cannot be expected to understand what it is like to be the final point of reference or the one with whom the buck stops. Being a head teacher in any school was quite a lonely position because it was difficult to be personally friendly with the staff that had to be managed. Other members of staff viewed such friendships dismally.

In the state system many support groups existed for head teachers and these were places where good friendships were established, problems shared and views aired. In the Independent sector it was much lonelier as a head because local colleagues were competitors and, when vying for pupils, it was not appropriate to share your success or trials with those who were market challengers. National associations were, and still are, very supportive to heads in the Independent sector but they are sometimes based far from schools.

In Luton, 70% of pupils in the school were from different ethnic minorities and for almost all these children English was their second language. I learned very quickly of the many cultures they represented, of what was important in their lives and of how the environment we provided could meet their needs and at the same time respect their upbringing. It was an exciting learning curve for us all and our lives were enhanced by the new experiences and new friendships that ensued in this quest.

We were very fortunate to have excellent bi-lingual support from the local authority in addition to helpful bi-lingual parents who came into school and assisted pupils. This enabled the children to think and feel secure in their home language as they developed their skill in the use of English and it made a colossal difference to their confidence and good integration. The effective communication we built up with parents led to trusting and productive relationships between home and school that were a positive influence upon children's learning.

I recall with great affection the colourful and bright Diwali days we had when staff and I dressed in the finery brought by the parents, ate the gorgeous sweets they made and lit special lamps.

Harvest too was a wonderful time as the parents joined us and watched our Christian celebration. We learned to understand, respect and acknowledge each other's differences in a safe and secure environment and our lives were made so much the richer for it. We valued each other as much as we valued ourselves. The children came to school in the dress that represented their way of life and parents were sensitive to the school by ensuring that such dress was in the school colours, so enabling all to feel a sense of shared community.

I spent a long while sorting out an agreement to obtain subsidy for daily milk provision and we were able to give children a third of a pint for a few pence each week. One day a very irate father came storming into my office. His threatening demeanour warned me that he was not a happy man. I was correct. He came right up to me and told me that if I asked him to send 20p a week for milk again for his child, he would thump me. When I asked him why, he calmly told me he could steal the milk for nothing. Not quite the answer I had expected. He was very aggressive and had I not been faster than him, I think he would have floored me there and then.

In order to protect me and make sure he did not have the same opportunity a second time, I took my Doberman, Lady, to school with me. Lady was a big dog with a fierce bearing; however she was absolutely lovely with the children. She could sense aggression at a hundred paces and if she did, she looked and sounded especially nasty. The word soon got around the neighbourhood. I was never bothered again and the dog could return to her usual job of protecting the house.

At this time, we had a very sad and shocking incident in the school with a lovely child who had signs of abuse. We followed all the correct procedures and eventually the case went to court. The paperwork for such cases is extensive and the time required to complete checks enormous. However, both parents claimed responsibility for such abuse and received probation. They took the child from the school and moved to another town. We could never forget the child and I have never forgiven myself at failing her. This spurred me to become very interested in such cases and I introduced a multi-agency team that met regularly to discuss cases that were only of slight concern, so that they could be sorted out, assisted and resolved before they turned into major concerns. It worked exceptionally well and each agency respected the work and guidelines of the other.

The school was in a tough area surrounded by families with problems who lived, often, in sub-standard housing. So much so, that one afternoon the police asked me to lock the school doors until they gave me the 'all clear.' The 'all clear' for what, I enquired? Well, the house adjacent to the school was 'a scene of crime' apparently. An argument between drug dealers had erupted and one had been shot within yards of the school door. In such as situation you do not worry, you just get on with it.

Another day, we had a phone call telling us that a bomb was planted in the school. 'Oh', I said. Then the penny dropped. I had a few quiet and personal moments of panic, went to the toilet, and then put all the necessary procedures into place. We emptied the school speedily, the children had extra games on the field and the deputy and I helped the police search. It was only after ten minutes that it suddenly occurred to me that if there was a bomb, why was I searching? I valued my life too much to give it away. So I informed the police I hoped their search was successful and my deputy and I would be on the field if they wanted us. Of course, there was no bomb, but this was at the height of the time when the IRA was active in England and a good many Irish supporters lived in the area.

Many children came to us without much language at all. Some could barely string a sentence together, few had any idea of what words or letters were. A large number suffered from malnutrition. We put a concentrated system of phonic teaching into place – very structured, very formal and very effective. We provided breakfast for the children, milk and biscuits at break and a good lunch that Jamie Oliver would have been proud of, the kind of thing the education secretary is thinking of introducing as a new idea in 2006. I so wish that Secretaries of State for education would give schools credit for the damn hard work they do now and have done over the years instead of using the system as a political football.

Many, many teachers have been using phonics to teach reading effectively for years, yet they have received little credit for their work. They were prevented from giving so much time to reading because the government insisted a hundred and one other things, as well as the basics, were introduced into the classroom. I really feel if we let teachers do their job, support them, give them the time and the materials and they will show every government how they can achieve results.

In Luton, I introduced a programme for children who had learning and behaviour difficulties and included parents, teachers, pupils and all local authority personnel in the programme. I then began to train staff from other schools and eventually we made a video for the local training college to use with their students and I wrote a book to accompany it. We had much fun doing this and learned a lot about filming that had us in absolute stitches. The most important thing I learned was that the media and I did not go well together.

Our basic premise was that every child is special and every child deserves the best. The fact is that the best is different for each child, so the class teacher has to discover what the best is, plan properly for it then provide it. The government has moved dramatically forward in provision for children with specific learning needs; however much is still to be done and, for some, provision is best given in specially designated schools. Through our work we proved deprivation could be overcome during the school day and not be an impossible problem to exciting learning. We organised an exhibition called 'Maths for fun' and filled the large school hall with magic and stimulating displays of children's work linked to maths. A fabulous huge, three-dimensional display showed how nature helped with tables. Giant ladybirds floated everywhere to assist with pattern and hideous spiders crawled up the woodwork doing their eight times table. The patterns used by children from other cultures gave us stunning, colourful examples of repeating and tessellating patterns. A school treasure trail organised by the children tested their parents' ability to recognise and use coordinates. It just went on and on. The children's enthusiasm was endless, harnessed by excellent and dedicated teachers. All the children contributed to a book of recipes that demonstrated their capability to use measurements, follow timings and record instructions accurately. The results were sold in the area to raise money for more equipment. Of course we got lots of publicity in the local press. This is important because it raises the status of the school and makes the population as a whole realise that schools are a valuable resource to the community.

Over the years, as these children grew and moved on to other schools, I often saw them in the local town if I stopped to collect groceries before going home. They would run up to me at the car park and tell me what they were doing, then proudly inform me they would guard my car free of charge and not let anyone put a finger on it. I was never sure whether to be pleased that the car was safe or embarrassed because I was condoning what could have been blackmail had I been an ordinary member of the public, as the youths asked for a financial contribution from the public for ensuring their cars came to no harm.

Schools in inner cities bring with them a myriad of problems that involve constant interaction with all types of public sector agencies. Parents, who are often unable to cope with the world or to ask for help when they need it, require support. As well as this, teachers require guidance to develop their careers; local authorities ask you to lead their training, children's work requires evaluating, school life needs monitoring regularly and the work piles up. One thing I did from day one as a head that has helped ever since was to keep a traffic light pad on my desk and by my bedside. All the vital tasks placed under red, urgent, were to be completed before I left for home, whatever the time. Tasks placed in the orange column were fairly urgent and to be looked at and completed, if possible, before I went home and anything in the green meant they could go and jump until I was ready for them. Often it is impossible to clear the mind of everything before going to sleep at night so if I woke up and thought of something, I simply wrote it down on the pad then I could happily go back to sleep. One local authority adviser told me of how he had a cricket bin by his desk when he was a head. When I asked what he meant, he said it was his LBW bin-let the b****** wait.

I also stopped answering the telephone myself and left this to my exceptionally efficient secretary who noted down all calls as they came in. Between certain times of the day, usually times when the school was working quietly (are there ever such times?) I would return all the calls. This freed up so much of my time for actual schoolwork.

During these years, we spent family holidays in Brynsiencyn on Anglesey at the cottage my parents had bought, because we simply could not afford a posh holiday. My parents paid for our children to go abroad with their schools and for the many treats that they had. The cottage was close to glorious beaches that the children loved and their father played happily with them and their dinghy in the sea for hours on end. There was still much to do to get the house into a reasonable state, but we divided our time between doing this and spending lots of time enjoying ourselves.

I have to tell you that we were often surprised at village life. City dwellers have nothing on villagers. We were burgled and all the coins stolen from the meter. We reported this to the local police house and the policeman greeted us with the words, -'Ah, I was waiting to see who it was he had done, okay I'll go and sort it out.' The culprit had been spending the coins in the local shop and the shopkeeper told the policeman. How different to now when, if there is a problem, you ring a number and eventually get connected to a policeman miles away.

When we first visited the village there was a post-office, a bank, a butcher, a Co-op, a hairdresser and a haberdasher. No need for villagers to leave and the daily gossiping could be done as the groceries were collected. Now there is the Spar, the post office, the chip shop and nothing else. The heart of village gossip has been removed. No wonder people leave. Our house was on the village high street and on more than one occasion merry villagers, coming home from the local pub, have forgotten their driving skills and smashed into the dining room. We had a good relationship with the local builder and he always sorted it out for us. In fact on one occasion someone knocked the lamppost by the house, the top fell into our roof and it was repaired before we knew anything about it. Villagers stick together.

Village life in Wales is much the same as village life in England, but in a different language. Each village has its colourful characters and its feuds. The week in a village revolved around routines. Monday was washing day, Thursday was market day in the island town and Sunday is, of course, either Chapel or Church. It matters a lot whether you are Chapel or Church and the congregations of each kept their distance. Both were recognisable by their Sunday suits and pretty hats, straw in summer and felt in winter.

In the village everyone knew everyone else. Little old ladies watched sneakily through their pristine nets to monitor movements through the main street, old men sat brazenly at the pub in positions where they saw everything that was happening. In Wales the name Jones is similar to Smith in England. In most villages at that time you could find a Jones the bread, Jones the baker, Jones the post, Jones the fish, Jones the coal etc, etc. In fact, the story goes that one day when a stranger came to the village he was perplexed by this plethora of Jones'. He had been asked by the security agencies to make contact with an undercover member of the organisation in the village called Jones. He was in such a quandary he decided to try the post office first so in he went, leaned over the counter, and said 'the daffodils are brown today' to the postmaster. Back came the reply, 'Oh, it'll be Jones the spy you want, try the – first house after the bank!

One year the local council caused much dissension amongst the locals as they wanted to erect a block of public toilets in the village. Whenever our family arrived we were inundated with folk supporting different sides of the argument trying to obtain our signatures. Diplomacy dictated that this required abstention. Each group was vehement in their views and the whole thing escalated into a hilarious argument with villagers who had been friends for years not speaking to each other. Eventually the council erected the block, but in a place that did not interfere with anyone's view of the magnificent scenery beyond.

The village knew who we were and, because of my husband's job, they were kind and helpful. One family, who lived opposite us, contained a plethora of colourful and unusual characters. It was impossible to pass the house without hearing arguments, drunken swearing or other unusual noises. We received a phone call one day from the elderly father to tell us he had run away from home and asking us to let his wife know. He was over sixty and had just legged it. My husband put his collar on and carefully told the wife the content of the phone call. We then left them to it. Needless to say, their comments could be heard far and near.

Time in a village, especially a Welsh village, is not Greenwich time but Welsh village time. Hours are slower, days are longer and estimates for completing work are unreal. Nothing is ever finished at the designated time. All the locals understood this. We did not but over the years, we learned. The best way of explaining it is to recall the occasion when asking a local villager if the Welsh have a word similar the Spanish ' manyana' and back came the answer – 'Oh, no, boyo, nothing with the same sense of urgency.' So, we interspersed life in a suburban community with holidays in a village community. The cottage in Brynsiencyn was an escape for us where we could be ourselves. No one could contact us and the hours of the day were ours to control.

The work in Hemel Hempstead continued, developed and extended and was very successful. However, nothing lasts forever. We had been very fortunate to be able to remain in this 'living' for a long time, but, of course, all good things must come to and end and the powers to be felt that it was time for us to move on.

CHAPTER 6
Life Changes

Well, we were on the move again. On this occasion we did not move far, just a few miles to Watford, the place that is the far outpost of civilisation for all Londoners and beyond which nothing exists for them. I could remain in my post and my friends were still close by. It was another stimulating experience as Henry was invited to take charge of a modern and innovative city church in an exciting building.

Our children were now at prep school in Watford and loving it (paid for by my parents). Naomi was the outspoken, gregarious, creative and interesting child and Christopher the quiet, imaginative, well behaved and gentle child. Both were fabulous kids who achieved well at school. When they moved to senior school, I remember being called from my office to their head's office as Naomi was in trouble for hitting someone who was bullying her brother. The head was very sympathetic, but rules are rules. Christopher was never bullied again – rough but effective justice I think.

The Watford church provided us with excellent accommodation in Cassiobury Park, a very lovely area. We could never have afforded to live in such a peaceful, leafy area and it was safe for the children. The house was the best cared for in our lives in the church so far. It was regularly decorated, repairs were fixed and, without us asking, the church committee would upgrade the provision annually.

The 'lady' from the previous church, who had tried to become a favourite of my husband, stuck her nose in as we moved. She came to see my new house without my knowledge.

This time I was not let down by my psychic powers as I sensed what had happened. One day I felt a strong urge to walk along to the church and sure enough, she arrived to see my husband. He was not there but I was, so I exchanged a few kind words with her. When asked what her husband thought about her behaviour, she seemed to disappear from sight somewhat and never reappeared.

As always I helped Henry and put as much energy as I could into supporting him, whilst developing my own career. This town church was exciting. It was an original and innovative building, just on the edge of the town in a leafy and pleasant area. Within the congregation were many well-motivated, forward thinking, intelligent and thoughtful people. A sports hall with its own changing room and shower facilities was attached, a well-appointed youth centre, a superb stage and hall with rooms for the actors, large kitchens and a modern space for a worship centre. This was the type of building that served God and mammon and allowed the church to be different, stimulating and to reach out to the community and beyond. The congregation were primarily professional people and really appreciated my husband's ministry. Slowly the church grew and expanded in numbers and vision.

I built a burgeoning career as a lecturer at this time, training teachers to take charge of and organise provision for special needs in their primary schools. I also obtained a headship at a large primary school with a nursery in Yiewsley, another St Matthew's. I was in my element. I loved it. This time I was in a church school. Seems I couldn't get away from the church, even at work. I became a commuter and travelled to and from work along the M25, learning to anticipate the traffic surges that suddenly appeared then disappeared just as mysteriously.

This was a very happy school with a long history; much of which had been documented in old logbooks. Wonderful stories existed of how the children were taken to the shelters during bombing raids and kept amused with community singing. In every community interesting things happen and this was no different. One day we discovered a pupil to be a member of a family linked to national security concerns, and the police escorted the child to and from school. The little girl was related to the people responsible for placing the bombs into a night-club in Berlin and then sending a person onto a plane at Heathrow with, unbeknown to her, a bomb in her luggage. The paparazzi appeared at the school and on the telephone and after this experience I have considerable sympathy for the Royals. We had suddenly become interesting to the media, not for the great work being undertaken by the dedicated and talented staff, but because a child connected with a terrorist attended. The reporters treated us with disdain and hassled us heartlessly until the child was removed to a safe place.

I assisted the local authority with the training of newly qualified teachers and thoroughly enjoyed this. It never failed to surprise me how little they had been taught about actual classroom organisation and survival. They were very conversant with educational theory but when it came to organising the class, knowing how to attract the children's' attention and persuade the children to do as they were told when they were told, the young teachers had been left to their own devices. Some were naturals and swam immediately. Others struggled, paddling furiously beneath the surface, however with a few relevant aids and tips here and there they gained their confidence and took off from the side to swim happily!

The things I stressed to these new teachers as being vitally important were preparation, organisation and expectations, in other words know what they were going to teach, have it well organised and planned, and always expect the highest standards of every child. I often felt teachers were like actors really, they have a story to tell and they want a good reaction.

As a head teacher it is always a thrill to walk around the school and hear the buzz of learning in the classrooms, the clattering exchanges of ideas and the fascination of watching children extend their knowledge. I so enjoyed it when the children came to explain to me what they were doing. They demonstrated how clearly they understood the tasks because their teachers had given them challenges eminently suited to their needs and abilities.

On some occasions, however, it was clear that a few teachers still 'told' children what they should know, instead of enabling the children to find out information and acquire knowledge for themselves. Only by allowing a child to think creatively, to explore ideas and to deduce his or her own conclusions will real and lasting learning take place and individual, creative and unique ideas be produced.

I loved having the opportunity to do assemblies. It is amazing how spiritual and moving assemblies with young children can be. The youngest children have a vision of the world uncluttered by political correctness or by adult perceptions. It is often as true a picture of the world as you will hear or see anywhere and as adults we should take serious consideration of such words.

School hymn practices are the bane of many a music teacher's existence but they can be great fun. I loved to lead them as this gave me an opportunity to keep contact with all the children. I began with games that improved breathing techniques, then played with tongue twisters to sharpen the children's pronunciation and we usually ended up with our body orchestra that resulted in gales of laughter. Have you ever tried making sounds with parts of your body – acceptable ones that is – and putting them together as an orchestra would? I do confess I love teaching children to sing and it is what I miss most now. Children love singing if it is fun, if it challenges them and if you keep a fast pace throughout. I loved to send them back to class on a high and then watch as the poor staff got them to settle down to mathematics.

When a head, I sat in lessons regularly and I found that the teachers who captured pupils' attention most easily were those who spoke clearly and distinctly. Just occasionally, when I heard a teacher using too many colloquial expressions I stopped them.

Many people, who find themselves in the media spotlight, from footballers to film stars, could learn this lesson. They have a responsibility to their youthful followers whose money they happily receive.

This was the time of the ICT revolution and there was plenty of local authority training, which we all used to maximum effect. We had a great time being total 'cabbage fingers' but slowly we gained the skills we needed to teach. You see, children have no pre-conceptions of technology, to them it is a toy and they love toys. They experiment fearlessly whereas we try things out guardedly, scared we will make a mistake or break something. Many state schools were exceptionally fortunate to be kitted out with fabulous, new, state of the art ICT suites, but staff skills did not match the equipment. Sad to say a few teachers turned their faces to the wall, rather than find out the fantastic possibilities opening up to them through use of this media.

We worked hard with various behaviour programmes in this school to help a few pupils who found it difficult to conform. It took much time but was worth the struggle. The most effective were those used in parallel by parents and teachers at home and school.

I gave a high priority to courtesy, a strong moral code and a good dollop of culture during lessons. The children enjoyed contributing to classroom rules. They had a strong sense of justice. Their views were often totally politically incorrect but usually quite perceptive.

I was always sad when I found that parents did not teach their children simple courtesies such as 'please' and 'thank you,' or show them how to use a knife and fork. It is not the children's fault if they lack good manners and I used to tell the parents so. I organised parenting classes to help young parents who simply did not know how to bring up children. As the parents' confidence in us grew, they shared their concerns and their hopes and fears and we shared our knowledge and experience with them and very good partnerships and trust grew out of this.

We invited local nurses to talk to the parents about children's ailments and how to deal with them, we asked local health workers to talk about nutrition and good diet and we asked local authority workers to talk to parents about benefits and who to contact if they had money problems. It may seem unusual that we did this, but the relationships that built up added significantly to the personal development of the pupils at home and at school.

I enjoyed helping young teachers to map out a career plan, to identify their strengths and be aware of how they needed to improve. It seemed to me that the best teachers watched for innovative educational ideas, became conversant with them and used them, increasing their skills. I was delighted that many of them from my school gained promotions.

The children in the area surrounding the school had few holidays so we decided to organise visits to the Isle of Wight. These were great fun. I went on a few of them and ever since I have admired teachers who help on a school holidays. It is a worry from beginning to end. Teachers never relax because they are always conscious of their responsibility to the children. Of course, taking pupils away for a week or a few days is a great time for teachers and pupils to learn about each other. At this time the musical 'Grease' was a big hit and, on a week away for older pupils, I remember lots of children and staff trying to outdo each other dancing away to the music. The thing was, the children were just as energetic the next day but the teachers were rather stiffer. We also took parents with us so we learned to live as an extended family.

I was very fortunate here to be given the opportunity to attend a management-training course at a large manufacturing business with a few of my colleagues. This was some of the best training I have ever received and opened up a whole new world for me. The funniest experience was solving a problem using lego while in a group with three male colleagues. I was pushed to the edge of the group as using lego and manipulating it was clearly a 'man's job.' So, I watched them tussle and argue and try to resolve it. As they worked it occurred to me how they could finish the exercise but, because they were disagreeing so much they could not see how easy the solution was. When they paused, I took some lego and placed it in the right position and the problem was solved. I must admit we ached with laughing when they realised what had happened.

The biggest lesson for the businessmen was that children couldn't be treated the same as commodities. This is because in a class there are 22 different items, each made up of different ingredients and each reacting to different stimuli in their own way, even though the packaging, their uniform, may look the same. This was an eye-opener to the businessmen and they confessed they would not know where to start with the children!

Many local authorities offer really interesting opportunities to heads to develop and I worked with a group of staff to provide material on possibilities for changing the timing of the school day. This was innovative work but the general public was not ready for such ambitious ideas.

My first contact with Aids occurred in this headship. This was a very new experience and we had to find our way carefully and with much help from medical authorities. A beautiful little girl, who was adopted by a loving family, had been born with the disease due to the addiction of her parents. Of course we had to learn as much as we could about the illness, about the difference between HIV and Aids and about the special techniques for handling bodily fluids etc, all of which are second place in schools now.

This situation again brought me into positive contact with many other agencies such as social services, health authorities and the police community liaison officers. It became very clear that such multi-agency work was vitally important to ensuring smooth and productive relationships between school, home and the community. As a result, we set up regular multi-agency meetings to discuss all types of issues and to learn about each other's work. This enabled us to deal with small difficulties before they grew and, should major problems occur, we knew all the necessary personnel to be contacted.

CHAPTER 7

Who Am I?

Whilst I spent happy days, months and years in this school, family life moved on. My mother contracted cancer of the oesophagus during this time and began a valiant but unsuccessful fight against this brutal aggressor. She accepted strong chemotherapy and bravely fought off the sickness that followed because she so desperately wanted to live. Although doctors warned us that her time was limited to a maximum of three months, her iron will enabled her to manage another eighteen. Her courage and determination were a beacon to those around. We never once heard her complain. I wanted to travel north to see her most weekends and the children of course wanted to see their grandmother who they adored.

One of the disadvantages of being 'called' to different parts of the country is that you are often far from your parent's home and in times of urgency, this can be difficult. It also means that very little family support is available as the children grow up. Whilst other families may have parents to look after children whilst they go out, this was a luxury we had to manage without. Consequently I was always a member of baby-sitting circles in the areas we lived, as these were a saving grace on many occasions.

The staff at St. Matthew's were wonderful when my mother was ill; they supported me in a way I could never have hoped for. My deputy was a tower of strength, jobs were done before I asked about them and work was completed before it reached my desk. After a vigorous battle during which she fought bravely against the dying of the human light my mother passed away quite suddenly in hospital one Friday morning, which surprised us all. As I arrived at school at the usual 7.40 am I received a phone call from the hospital to tell me she had died. The school caretaker made me sit down, gave me a cup of tea and worried over me. I drove speedily from school to home without remembering the journey. I was so very angry with my mother for not waiting for me to get there. How could she die on her own? Why had I let her down by not being there? It took me a long time to come to terms with this. I remember shouting as I drove, about how unfair life was and how I was not ready to be left on my own, whilst negotiating traffic lights through tear-filled eyes.

My father was devastated, as he could not accept her illness never mind her death so I had to deal with everything. Henry was a rock; he knew exactly what had to be done. I remember visiting my mum at the Chapel of Rest. I saw this tiny lady who had been so great and warm in life, now such a cold, small and still body. It was clear that her soul, that which made her the person I knew, was no longer in this shell. Where had it gone, I wondered? I cried and said I had no one left, but Henry reassured me that he would always be there for me.

One evening shortly after my mother died, I awoke to see her above the bed and I knew then that she would always look after me and this was her way of telling me. I was not in the least frightened.

After my mother's death I returned to work to be met by a kind and caring chairman of governors. He was very solicitous and told me that he knew I could cope with the situation, because I had a faith and because I was head of a church school. In his own way I knew he was being very kind and supportive but I longed to tell him I actually hated God, I did not believe in Him, He had mucked up my whole life and as far as I was concerned He could get lost. But of course I did the clergy wife smile and thanked him for his concern. You see, there is no avenue for a clergy wife with doubts and grief to go down, especially when head of a church school. She has to be a shining example of faith to the flock!

I did a silly thing then, I worked myself into the ground so that I did not have time or space to think about my loss. This was great for the school because we were very ambitious. The staff gained many promotions and the school was used for many initiatives and training meetings. I wrote and led training courses on the curriculum, management, special needs and counselling in education.

However, this was not really good for me or for my family. Henry simply stayed in the background and watched, ready to catch me when, inevitably, I fell. My caring and exceptionally supportive deputy-head could also see what was happening and was ready to pick me up if I needed it. Between them, Henry and Mick just let the steam burst from my seams and waited until the explosion. Of course it surely came, after a few months.

Those of you who have suffered any kind of trauma will, I am sure, recognise the symptoms. One morning on the way to the car, I shouted the usual good-byes to the family and jauntily opened the front door to a glorious day. As I stepped outside something very peculiar happened. What was wrong, I thought. I tried to put a foot out again and nothing happened. It was as if my legs were turned to stone. I simply could not go outside. My brain was sending the right messages, but my body was not responding. Was I having a stroke? Was I going mad? No, my body was simply reacting to all the hell it had been put through in the previous few years, exacerbated by my mother's death.

I was the only person it seemed, who was not surprised by this state of affairs. Henry contacted our excellent doctor who knew exactly what was happening. He sent me to bed for my body to rest and then helped get my mind and my rocketing blood pressure sorted out. I spent a lot of time crying when the children were at school and tried to pull myself together for the time they came home. I shouted at God, at my husband, at everything.

Why should I be left so alone, why should I be treated so badly by the world? Strangely enough, no matter how deep I fell I could not get to the bottom and this also angered me. It seemed as if my mother or God were there stopping me from finally sinking irretrievably into the morass. That also annoyed me, because I wanted to sink. Slowly, very slowly I recovered strength and emerged again into the world. Each day I gave myself small targets. My first was to walk to the end of the road, holding on to Henry's arm. He was the essence of patience. I remember vividly hanging on to him as I pushed one foot before the other in order to reach the local shop. When I got there, I could not go inside so I had to go through the same agony getting back to the house.

The next goal was to walk into the town with Henry and have a coffee in Trewin's. Again he supported me very strongly. On many occasions, I wanted to give in and stay in. However, the more I persevered the better I got. I had excellent, simple advice from a colleague who was also a skilled counsellor. He told me not to give in, to keep going even if I failed. He was right.

To drive the car was the final major step forward. I sat in it for a long time, as I couldn't remember what the controls were for. Henry quietly and patiently took me through everything again. He supported me fantastically, even though he was terror stricken sitting in the car on that first journey I made. This was not a good time. I expect many of you know what I mean when I say I would be in the middle of a shop and the iron fist of panic would grip and turn in my chest for no reason at all. It would then begin a mad and erratic thumping within me and take hold of my breath. Many times, I just had to drop the groceries and run. I lost weight, sleep and confidence.

I don't think I have ever been quite as strong or confident as I was before this time, but I am more understanding of others and of how life experiences may affect them at work and at home.

When you have children a part of you knows that, no matter what, you simply have to get going again. But it was a struggle. Friends were fantastic and let me say what I needed to say and made no judgements, just supported. Henry supported me very well. I made progress and got going again, but would never again be the same person deep down, for such a situation changes your innermost being.

My experience helped me to consider how others in similar situations are assisted, particularly children, and of just how little skilled help is often available for children in schools. So I signed up to undertake a post-graduate diploma in counselling in London and was allowed one day a week to attend the course that lasted two years, on condition I used the skills in the local authority. I considered this a very good deal. It was great attending lectures again and looking into a new area of learning. Meeting a completely different range of people was also interesting.

Another aspect of the course involved a complete self searching of attitudes, feelings and developing the ability to express innermost thoughts to other people. This was very hard, especially for me, as underneath the confident exterior lurks and always has lurked a very shy person with little confidence. However, I learned to share things I never thought it possible to share and these burdens became lighter and less important simply for being shared and held by others. The skills and techniques I became conversant with were extremely useful in school and we adopted many in our pastoral care work.

I think this post-graduate course, together with the counselling study I was to do later as part of a Masters degree, have been the most useful and productive studies I have ever undertaken. The skills have been particularly useful with concerned and worried parents. We professionals often forget that parents are actually scared of schools, are fiercely protective of their children and listen to stories of school life through the eyes of their children. When parents then come into school to sort out the problem their fear takes over and they either become very quiet and passive or very loud, obstinate or aggressive. Knowing how to discover what their behaviour is hiding is enormously useful. It takes away the anger and enables constructive dialogue to begin.

Another shock awaited me following my mother's death, something I could never have dreamed may happen. My father told me that, when my grandmother had died, my mother found her own birth certificate and discovered that she was adopted soon after birth. This had shaken my mother considerably and I do not think she ever recovered. She had kept the information hidden but of course it was now out in the open. At the time, I put it to the back of my mind and left it there out of respect for my mother's wishes. She had never searched for her real family. She told my father that in the back of her mind, all through her life, she wondered if there was something not quite genuine about her family. As a child she had occasionally been taunted about being 'different'. This fell into place on her discovery.

It seemed as if a whole part of my history, my family foundations and the people who had been most close to me had suddenly collapsed around me. I left the situation alone for many years but later in life, after Naomi was married, I realised how important it was to understand our place in the family history, so I made the decision to try and trace any birth relatives of my mother that may still be alive.

Tracing relatives is not as easy as it sounds, primarily because you usually begin with so little information and then encounter many frustrating twists and turns along the way. It seems to me that the further back you wish to go the easier it is. When it comes to finding possible living relatives, then matters take a totally different turn. I found out who my real grandparents were with relative ease, a Jemima and Norman-Storey Todd from Baxter Avenue in Newcastle, using the information on my mother's birth certificate to scour the registers of marriages, births and deaths. Then I discovered there were three other children, two girls and a boy, born to them after my mother. This came as a tremendous shock, for it then made me wonder why a couple should give away a first baby and then go on to have other children. Further research informed me that my great-grandparents, as well as my grandparents, were Master Draper's. Census forms showed they lived in a spacious house with servants and a governess. My grandfather was one of their sons. My mother was born to my grandfather and his wife only four months after they married. In those days this was probably regarded as a social calamity and I suspect it is possible that grandparents could have been pressured to give the baby up for adoption.

I cannot help but wonder if my grandparents ever remembered, at various times of their lives, the daughter they gave away. For example, did they ever take a moment to think of her at the anniversary of her birth, or at Christmas? Did they ever wonder what had happened to her or did they know what had happened to her? Did they want to see her before they died? Surely a mother could not be so unfeeling as to forget her first-born? The strange thing is they lived just half a mile from the couple who adopted my mother for quite a few years so I cannot help wondering if they ever saw my mother and watched her progress.

I decided to try to trace the other children, who would be my mother's two sisters and brother. These people would be my aunts and uncle. I have no brothers or sisters and I believed my mother to be an only child also and then here I was, suddenly being faced with the prospect of having aunts, an uncle and possibly cousins. My father had been an only child so I had no relatives from that side of the family. This new information was a lot to absorb. It felt very strange. Did I really know who I was?

I obtained the birth certificates for my aunts and uncle and from there I looked for their death certificates but two of these did not exist, so I realised they must both still be alive. One daughter had died in childhood. I then looked for marriage certificates and found that when my aunt had married in Yorkshire she was living with my grandparents at the time, so for whatever reason the family had moved there. My grandfather was then the steward at Wetherby Golf Club. I then traced my grandparents' deaths. These were registered by my uncle in Aylesbury, so they had moved yet again. When living in Buckinghamshire my mother's family had been living only a few miles from Henry and me in Hemel Hempstead.

I soon realised that searching for relatives requires time, patience and money. There is usually a cost to every search and certificate you need. In the end, although I was spending a considerable amount I was getting nowhere. I decided to enlist the services of a people tracing agency. I found the name and details of one from the internet that had been used by television companies. For an initial payment and providing all the details found to date, I left them to find my uncle. The cost only covered a search for one person, but I reasoned that if I found an uncle, he would probably know where an aunt lived. I was allocated a researcher and it took him over a year to come up with very vague information for me which consisted of a possible address for my uncle abroad. Following my experience I think I would advise anyone intending to use such an avenue, to find out exactly what is provided before signing up.

I was given an address abroad so now the search was in a country hundreds of miles away. I believed my uncle to reside on an island in the Western Mediterranean. I decided to visit every imaginable web-site for the island and one thing is for sure, the address I had been given did not exist. Now it occurred to me that many times during his ministry, Henry received letters from folk trying to trace their relatives and asking for his assistance. So I thought to myself, let me see if I can find a church contact in the area that I am searching. I discovered a great web-site for the Anglican Church. It was informative, colourful and showed how active the church was in the area. It also had details of the vicar. I took a big breath and sent the vicar the name and possible area in which I believed my uncle resided and asked if he could help me with an address or phone number. Within 24 hours he replied with a phone number in that area. As he said in his email, it probably was the same person as it was not likely two English people with that name would be residing in the area I had given.

Now it is one thing searching and wondering and following a trail. It is quite another having an actual contact number. This could be the start of a new and exciting journey or it could be a dead end or it could be both the beginning and the end of a journey with folk who really do not wish to know about the past. After all, the chap in question must be in his late seventies and I did not wish to do any damage to his constitution. I sat for ages toying with the possibilities. What do they look like, these family members who know nothing of my mother or me, do we have any family resemblances. What kind of lives have they lived? I put the number away and let the thoughts remain in my mind to gain a focus on what I was doing. I knew deep down that the only way to satisfy my yearning and find out what was going to happen was to pluck up the courage and make the phone call.

Well, it happened that I felt lousy the few days after receiving the phone number. I had a stinking summer cold, goodness only knows where I picked it up but I felt dizzy, breathless and very snotty. I could use this as a good excuse for not ringing. The trouble was that when I was better I might find another excuse. In the end I sat down, picked up the phone and dialled. It takes a few seconds to be connected to another country and the dialling and ringing tones are different. The phone was answered with a 'Yes?' Now this is never an easy introduction to a conversation. The first thing I did was to establish the identity of the recipient, then I simply had to launch in.

I explained that I had been researching my family history and believed it was possible that we were related and asked if he was willing to spend a few minutes trying to help me. Clearly I was talking to a very nice gentleman because he said of course he would listen. I asked for details about his mother and father and they matched the details of my real grandparents exactly. I had no alternative but to say I thought he was my uncle and his parents were my grandparents. I explained what I had found out and he was just as shocked as I had been. But the facts I gave were so accurate he realised there was something to this conversation.

I told him a little about myself and he told me that his sister, my aunt, lived just four miles away from him. She had four children, who would be my cousins. As an only child I can remember how many times I had longed for cousins to play with and talk to, envying my friends who seemed to have so many.

I gave him my phone number and email address and he said he would ask his sister to contact me. I copied my mother's birth certificate and sent photographs of my mother at various stages throughout her life to see if they could spot any family resemblance. I also wrote a short summary of her life for them and told them a little about myself. I posted the information, with a sincere wish that it would reach sensitive hands. I waited with anticipation to hear about my family.

About three weeks after I sent this information, I received a large brown envelope. In it was returned all the information and photographs, excepting the letter and copy of the birth certificate, which I had sent. Also there was a brief family medical summary. No letter, no other correspondence. It seemed pretty clear that they did not wish to have anything to do with me, which was very hurtful. I realise it is not their fault that they had a sister they did not know about, but neither is it my fault. I do appreciate that they must be as shocked as my mother and I were on learning of these facts and probably wondering what on earth I want. Actually, I want a photograph of my grandparents and a little information about them. Part of me thinks they probably see me as their skeleton in the cupboard and they want to keep the cupboard door shut. Tough, once the skeleton is out there is no going back.

I was alarmed to read the family medical history. A significant occurrence of breast cancer throughout the family is quite unnerving to say the least and other cancers have also surfaced here and there. My experience does stress the importance of knowing and understanding family medical histories so that we can either adapt our own lifestyles or make suitable arrangements to monitor health. 'Dupytrens' was also common in family members. I suppose they are in good company here, depending on your point of view, as this is what Margaret Thatcher suffered from and had to have a small operation to correct. It is when the connective tissue in the palm thickens and restricts movement of the fingers. In some ways I wish I had never found this out.

I contacted the family again and requested further details connected with medical histories. I again requested a photograph of my grandparents and some information about what they did, where they lived and why they moved around the country. The aunt and uncle were courteous enough to send the requested medical information. Alongside this was attached half a sheet of typewritten paper that informed me how they wished to have nothing to do with me or my family and any further communication from me would be destroyed unopened. I cannot begin to tell you how wretched this made me feel. The note was not addressed to anyone nor signed by anyone. Deep down I feel that if this is the sort of people my relations are, then I actually do not wish to know them either, but I will not give up.

CHAPTER 8

Land of the Celts

Late summer is a lovely time of the year. The slow, heavy and misty grey mornings often give way to warm, golden sunshine. The remnants of luscious, juicy, fruits hang gingerly on branches and squirrels greedily collect their larder for the forthcoming winter. In Watford our house had a very large garden and we enjoyed watching the squirrels beaver away gathering their food stores. In the spring these wretches couldn't remember where they had buried the nuts and spent days digging up the lawn to find them, much to Henry's horror and the torment of the dog.

Middle age had now arrived, a time when broadness of the mind and narrowness of the waist change places. Life had improved and appeared to be going quite well. We were working through Naomi's teenage years reasonably successfully, though by no means uneventfully. I have to say I prefer the 'terrible two's' any day. Having been head of a senior school and a mother of two, I can tell you that girls' teenage years are a living nightmare for their parents. If you say something is black, they are adamant it is white. If you like something, then it is diabolical in their eyes. You are an embarrassment to them; they want space, freedom, a life of their own, etc. At the same time as they are attempting to fit into adult bodies, a part of them is still a little girl and they try to manage the changes without falling on their faces. All we parents can do is listen, support, turn grey gracefully with the worry, be available when needed and try to hope that the principles instilled in the early years will take them through the storms. Personally, I found chats with friends who also had teenagers very helpful and immensely reassuring as it helped us realise we were not alone. The sense of release experienced over a glass of wine, whilst bemoaning the trials and tribulations of teenagers, was glorious.

However, as you know, when your guard is down and you feel things are going fairly well, life catches up with you quite unexpectedly and kicks you from behind when all in front seems fine. Henry received an invitation to consider a move to Rhyl, in North Wales, and he was seriously interested. Hell! I considered this to be the far end of civilisation. In hindsight, I really wish I had said no, I was not going. Naomi had to stay with our friends for a term to finish her studies, Christopher had to attend a local Welsh school that was nowhere near as good as his school in Watford and I had to find a new job. Our friends all thought we had taken leave of our senses and they were to be proved right.

I did not want to give up a very successful job in which I had made massive progress, though I felt that as a wife it was both my turn and my duty to follow my husband. It was a very hard and painful move and took place in a howling gale. The day after we left, in February 1990, one of the huge fir trees in the garden fell onto the garage of the house we had left. I could not but help wonder, was this some kind of omen perhaps?

We travelled North behind the removal lorry and were held up in an enormous traffic jam on the motorway, caused by the weather. We moved to the inside lane of the motorway as the lorries were lifting on their wheels because of the wind, and the last thing we needed was to find ourselves beneath one. The journey took eight hours, twice the expected time.

The week we arrived, the whole coastal area was flooded and, instead of living five minutes walk from the sea we lived three minutes walk from sea. We were not flooded but times were grim for those who were. The seas were magnificent from a distance but close up they were powerful and menacing and a lot of people suffered enormous hardship after the initial flooding. The smell left behind by a mixture of seawater and drainage is awful and the damage to belongings was even worse.

In this parish there were three churches. Not all the members had wanted us there, apparently a few felt that Henry was not the right person for the job. We were not told this, of course, and had been assured that the call to the parish was unanimous. The folk had every right to feel as they did and we totally respected such views. Had we been told the truth our lives may have taken a totally different direction. Many folk thought Henry had been asked to come to the area because he was a member of a certain 'society', whose clientele wore aprons and rolled up their trouser legs. Nothing could be further from the truth.

My skills were not really required here so I had less trouble being myself. Shortly after our arrival Henry was told that one church had experienced an active and dominant clergy wife and certainly did not want another. Another church preferred me to chair some meetings, open fetes and donate whenever there was a fund-raising event, otherwise keep out of the way. So I simply did what was expected.

The saving grace of the area was its outstanding beauty. It could not be denied that it was spectacularly stunning. The seascapes and mountain ranges blended together to produce rugged contrasts that altered their shape and hue according to the ever-changing skies above. We both loved the scenery and found solace in walks along the empty and spacious beaches and in the fresh and pure mountains. The countryside captured us and there is no way we would want to leave it now. Of course in each of the churches there were a few lovely folk who were warm and welcoming and helped us to settle into this strange new experience. Many people denigrate Rhyl as a 'kiss me quick' sea-side town and this is so unfair to the town. A small section of the sea-front does have this side to it, but it really is a small section. The majority of the town is lively, colourful, friendly and happy with a number of positive things going on and beautiful long and clean beaches for children.

I did not speak the language of this Celtic land and found difficulty in finding a job. There were no schools as large as that I had left, so I had to reconsider what I was going to do. I was told that, irrespective of my credentials and talents, I would have great difficulty in obtaining a headship. My previous Director of Education, who originally hailed from Porthmadog, intimated that the problem was two-fold. Firstly, I could not speak Welsh and governors regarded this as a vital requirement even though most schools taught in English. Secondly, I was a female and emancipation for females, it appeared, was late in arriving in this country. Also, what was implied but not actually said was that I was English.

It was suggested to me that I gave thought to moving to the independent sector of education, so I obtained details of a preparatory school in the area that was advertising for a head teacher. This was a different type of challenge. The governors, acting upon the advice of a school inspector, wanted the place turning around, upgrading and putting on the map so to speak. It was not an easy task. Some of the staff wrote to the governors before I arrived, giving lots of reasons why they did not want me to change anything. The governors stuck to their decision to go for change and I got stuck in. Changing systems is never easy. Sometimes folk are on side, sometimes not.

This job was extremely hard at first. Some of the 'old guard' disliked every change I introduced, they tried to scupper whatever they could and on occasion were just plain 'bloody-minded.' I realised why the governors needed an experienced head to do the job. Someone with less experience and knowledge would have been devoured alive. If I tell you that it would have been easier to break a block of concrete with a toothpick than to make some of them smile, it may give you a glimpse of what I was up against. My thorough training in other headships had prepared me well and I stuck it out.

The school trebled in size, the buildings were extended and redesigned and I gathered together a strong staff team and filled the school with happy pupils. It became known as a very good school. A supportive governing body that, like me, cared deeply about education and giving every child the best quality of schooling supported me strongly.

During my time at this school, I received an invitation to a Buckingham Palace Garden Party, which was a real thrill. I am still not sure why I received it. I think it was because I was the first lady chairman in the North-West area of the Independent Association of Prep schools and I had organised a good amount of staff training in the area. Henry came with me. We thoroughly enjoyed the occasion. It was interesting to watch the politics of the afternoon. When the courtiers came along the aisles of guests deciding who should meet a member of the Royal Family, they automatically assumed that Henry, a clergyman, was the main guest and I was accompanying him. What a nerve. Emancipation for women had still not reached the Palace which was strange really since Her Majesty is female.

The trials and tribulations that come free of charge with headship do tend to turn head teachers into somewhat boring, sombre and serious people. It is possible to break free occasionally and let a little of the real person emerge. So it was for me, when the time of the staff versus pupils rounders match came. I dressed top to toe as a clown, make-up, the lot. At first a deathly hush descended as staff and pupils looked in amazement and for a momentary second, I thought, 'Oh, my God. I've got it wrong.' Then the children began to cheer and all was well. I scored lots of rounders because the children were too busy looking at the costume to keep their eyes on the ball. Just as well as I am absolutely rubbish at rounders.

It was the custom in the senior part of the school for the staff to dress up for the Christmas dinner. Now dressing up in front of seniors is a different matter – they are acutely critical creatures. I turned myself into an outrageous punk for the evening and when I marched down the length of the dining hall to the high table; stamps of approval reassured me I had it right. What intrigued me most was the comment of a male member of staff, 'I didn't recognise you,' he said, 'you looked so young and with it.' As I thought about this, it occurred that he might have been trying to tell me I usually looked like a boring old fart, but I gave him the benefit of the doubt.

Henry battled on in the area as best he could, working exceptionally hard for little return. Until this ministry he was always a hospital chaplain and an extremely good one, helping all kinds of people in the most distressing circumstances. Here though, his lack of the national language prevented him from having such a position, a great sorrow to him and a great loss to many. Whilst we understood that a person with Welsh as their first language would feel happier receiving solace and comfort in their mother tongue when ill, a lot of people in the local hospital were English and speak no Welsh.

His preaching continued to be dynamic, but few in the churches commented on the services. Of course they may have thought it was rubbish but they could at least have said so. Occasionally, when he took his drums into church and I played keyboard for him they could not fail to praise him for the stirring worship he led. Nothing is more demoralising for the clergy than to go on week after week, year after year carefully preparing services, delivering them and receiving no response. This was the first time this had happened during his ministry; so we presumed it must be a 'Welsh' thing.

Henry has always had forward thinking ideas but he was way ahead of his time in this area of the country and found the struggle hard. He gave his all and his great strength was his pastoral care of others. He served them loyally and, on occasion, to the detriment of his family, but that's clergy life. He is by no means alone in that.

Living in a tithed house makes you a prisoner in so many ways, but when you are young your love for your husband stretches and envelops everyone and conquers all. When you are older, love is not so generously elastic, it does not always encompass all as before and can be a bigger pain in the neck than your arthritis and lingers for longer. In Wales, we were not so fortunate as in Watford or Liverpool. Here the tithed house was quite unsatisfactory for the job and it became an albatross around our neck. Those responsible for its upkeep did not touch it for years and we were left living in sub-standard accommodation. It occurred to us that even asylum seekers were put into better housing.

A strange thing happened every Sunday. A number of older members of the congregation suddenly paraded through our back gate, across the garden path and out of the gate that led into the church grounds. This saved them five minutes on their walk to the church. They were very sweet, but again it emphasised that the clergy are never fully in control of their lives or their homes or their supposedly private space.

When we moved here we placed Christopher in the local comprehensive school. This was a big mistake as many pupils disliked the English. There were bullies and, apart from a few friendly and decent souls, many pupils were diabolically behaved. Our son survived and the experience helped him learn to handle himself in the outside world. We helped him cope because the school was useless. It brought home to us personally the dramatic effect bullying can have upon children. The school made all the requisite noises but were completely ineffective in implementing actions to stop the situation.

As a head teacher I occasionally received rather strange requests to help out with family affairs. Many children have disjointed families, some living with their mothers and some with their fathers. This matter involved a child who lived with her father. Mr Smith was quite an interesting man in late middle-age who had travelled the world. He and his wife rarely spoke to each other and were vitriolic about each other when speaking to me. On occasion I became like the nodding dogs in the back of cars, I simply kept nodding through the tirades, and then listened to what the real message was. Mr Smith had a female friend, who we knew well as she collected the child regularly. Now it appeared that when this lady stayed at the house overnight the child had a habit of coming into the bedroom early in the morning and often interrupting, should I say, an 'intimate' moment. Mr Smith wanted me to talk to the child; to explain to her what was happening during the 'intimate' moment and why it was important that they were not disturbed.

It was useful that in my clergy wife existence I had learned, years ago, to laugh on the inside. This time I was not just laughing, I was crying and trying not to let my shoulders shake. I gently informed the father that I did not get involved in personal home matters and I was sure he had the experience and sensitivity to deal with the matter appropriately himself. I never asked what the outcome of his talk with his daughter was, needless to say.

One of the advantages of being head in this school was that, at times, attendance was required at the headquarters of the school trustees at the Draper's Hall in London, a beautiful building that belonged to an old and established London Guild. These occasions were very grand and supremely enjoyable. That is, except for one evening when the hospitality caught up with me somewhat. Few ladies attended these occasions as this was a predominantly male preserve. Over a sumptuous dinner with the most exquisite wines, conversation flowed freely across the table. The Madeira served was as sweet as honey and simply slid down the throat. I have to mention here that I do not normally imbibe at all, so it was a pleasure for me to taste such superb wines.

As the dinner came to a close the few ladies present rose to move to the anteroom. As I was about to stand I realised, with abject horror, that my brain was no longer connected to my legs and no matter how hard I instructed my legs to stand they would not obey. They had taken on a complete life of their own and were quite unwilling to move sedately in directions not usually associated with walking. Absolute panic overcame me. I turned to one of the governors who was sitting on my immediate left and whispered the problem in his ear. He smiled sweetly and whispered to the gentleman on my right. They each took an arm and virtually lifted me to the anteroom, without the need of legs at all. Since I am small and they were tall no one noticed. Or at least, to this day, I hope no one noticed.

The governors of this school were exceptionally supportive of the head, the pupils and parents and were a pleasure to work for. As many of them were incredibly busy, I was sometimes required to attend meetings in London. I never objected, as a trip to the big city was always welcome and I managed to have a little time left to spend in the shops after the meeting. On one occasion, I had to go to the House of Lords for a meeting and was really privileged to find myself allowed to sit in the chamber as a guest of one of the members of the House until he could leave. It was particularly fascinating as an Education Bill was being discussed. On more than one occasion during the debate I wanted to jump up and argue with them. When the governor was free he took me for lunch in the House of Lords dining room. The food was good, simple fare. I looked around as we talked and recognised many famous faces chattering away. In fact, the only non-famous person in the room was me.

My interest in counselling in education continued, as did my work with school management so I studied both further within a research degree. This was hard as I had to complete the studies as I worked, attending university at weekends. Although the counselling techniques I gained were extremely useful I realised that I could be a far more effective as a counsellor in a different school. It is very hard to counsel pupils in a school in which you are a teacher, head of year or head. The pupils cannot separate the expectations you have in these roles with the freedom of the counselling situation. After a couple of years I obtained my Master's Degree and decided enough was enough, I did not wish to have any more pieces of paper.

After many happy years the Trustees sold the school. After the initial changes were in place it was a good time for me to move on, something I had been thinking of for a while, however I will always have a special place in my thoughts for the fascinating people, loyal friends, stirring teachers and wonderful children I met over the years whilst in that school.

Teachers should never underestimate the effect that they have on a child's life. Many past pupils ring me or stop me in the street to tell me what they are doing and to reminisce about their time in my class. I receive post cards from all over the world giving me information about the adventures that past pupils are involved in. Their memories of school life are razor sharp and serve to underline the impact one teacher can have on the life of the child. If we multiply that by all the children ever in our classes then our influence on society is phenomenal! It is always a thrill to know past pupils are successful. Most are now professional and working their way through the echelons of medicine or education. Others are overworked and overpaid as plumbers or electricians or builders.

The worst experience for me is when a former pupil stops me to introduce me to their son or daughter and then proceeds to tell their own children about the time they were in my class. Do I feel ancient? Does winter follow autumn?

Christopher was married here in 2003 and has settled happily in the locality. I am not a gremlin; I made a pact with myself never ever to be a gremlin. I help when I am asked and I support if needed. I like my daughter-in-law. She loves my son and that is all that matters for me.

Naomi too has settled in the area, has married recently and is quite close by. When I watch my daughter I know that I will never die, for she is a double of me. She is feisty and fiercely independent. She is an inveterate giggler and when we are out shopping together, we can start each other off at the smallest thing. In some ways she is stronger and has the assertiveness that comes with her generation. She suffered abominably at the hands of male colleagues in her place of work with teasing, snide comments, and nastiness because she was a competent female. She coped, battled through and gained promotion. It has almost stopped and I suspect they now admire her for her outspoken honesty and toughness. I have been lucky to experience little of such male arrogance throughout my career.

Whilst here I had a recurrence of the back trouble that has niggled me throughout my life and, on being sent to the National Orthopaedic hospital, found that a defect that has been there from birth was responsible. I wish I could tell this to all the doctors who, over the years, have simply regarded my grumbling about pains in my back as a pain in their neck.

On arriving in Wales I was constantly tired and was advised to take the elixir of middle-aged ladies everywhere – HRT. After a couple of weeks I found energy I thought had been lost forever. I could keep going and do work, home, church and whatever else was asked of me. Hot flushes disappeared, windows could be closed; I could get through meetings without having to have 'comfort breaks' ostensibly for other people, but really for me. Later I realised that nothing is free or that wonderful in life. After ten years I came off HRT, under the doctor's direction. If you ever think of coming off this elixir remember there are consequences. Try to stop in winter as you will have enough hot flushes to keep you warm. Make sure you buy plenty of anti-wrinkle cream, as your skin will fry in the sun. Be prepared for anything then you will not be disappointed. Sometimes a few shakes return, but if you do some exercise you will think it is the effect of the exercise. The weight you put on when taking the wonder drug does not come off. I learned in meetings just to say 'is it warm in here or is it me?' Everyone laughed and opened the windows. Do not sit next to anyone you know to be taking HRT or their energy will make you feel sick. Only have cold drinks in company as they keep your temperature down. Do not have alcohol or within a very short time your face will resemble the beetroot in the salad.

Now another interesting facet of clergy life emerges. When you are poor and on the breadline everyone is sorry for you, they give you handouts, they sigh at your devotion and it makes them feel better as they drive away in their Chelsea tractors to their comfortable homes. Isn't it good that someone is suffering on their behalf?

However, when the wife works and earns a good salary the mood of some folk changes. Is this clergyman still accepting the expenses he is entitled to? Is he asking that his house be decorated even though this is, in fact, part of his salary? Is he expecting congregations to support him when he has a wife who is doing this very well? Clergy wives marry the men not the church and it is about time people understood that. If clergy wives happen to have good careers as I did, this is no reason for the church to hop on the back of their success and expect to be relieved of their obligations.

We have made a handful of dear friends here. We enjoy their company very much and appreciate their loyalty. They have been faithful and supportive in our tough times and always kept us smiling. We experience the same problems as them for we are of a similar age. We are all beginning to creak in the same places, we all need to 'call in' at motorway stops rather more frequently than when we were young. We find we are buying new houses, not for us, but for our children. We are being used as the local bank for loans by children who are trying to make a few pennies stretch unbelievably. We have to write lists when we go to the shops, not to stop us buying too much, but to help us remember exactly what we have to buy. We love going shopping with our children but their energy to keep going tires us. Did we once expend so much energy when shopping – I guess so.

Looking back, we both worked far too many hours here, a mistake easily recognised in hindsight. We both should have put ourselves more to the fore. Others should learn from our errors. Careers and employers can be ruthless taskmasters and drain every ounce of energy from those in their employ. We should not allow ourselves to be eaten up by them, everyone needs to make time to step back and see the bigger picture in which we as individuals need to be nurtured.

CHAPTER 9

A New Beginning

Autumn is my favourite time of the year. The trees are at their most beautiful, glowing with rich, deep and vibrant oranges, browns and reds as they are beginning the process of dying. The dappled sunshine peeking through these leaves brings to mind gleaming jewels of amber and fire opal. These are free gems from God's earth to appreciate without cost. Cold mornings give way to warm afternoons and tranquil evenings. This is rather like us really. This is the first time I think Henry has influenced me. You see every clergyman is haunted by the phrase 'life's like that.' I used to tease Henry no end if he got anywhere near using it in his sermons and here I am almost doing it myself. Never mind, I feel no guilt, so I'd better get on with it. I think we are to some extent like the autumn trees, as our life begins to ebb gradually into the final seasons our beauty grows and the treasures of the years are gathered together on our faces and in our minds. Or this is how I look at it now. I accept that because I am getting older, my view may be somewhat coloured. It takes us a little longer to 'get it together' in the mornings but we're firing on all cylinders by the evening.

Early autumn is fine but I don't much care for late autumn. This is a cold time with winter beckoning its icy fingers around the corner and everyone thinks about hibernating. It is a time when the leaves have almost fallen from the trees, the skies are often grey and the fields are bare. However, the frosty mornings can offer beautiful, intricate patterns on the lowliest and ugliest branches and the sun can glow with a deep orange that warms the sky. The leaves as they prepare to finally die become brittle and fragile and are at their most stunning and we catch our breath as we gaze at the myriad of beauty death brings with it. Beauty too can be found in us during this season; it is just beauty of a different kind and sometimes has to be looked for a little harder than in other seasons.

As we enter what is kindly termed 'late middle age' the bones are no longer as supple; they are thinner and we feel the cold more. For some of us osteoporosis and arthritis have appeared and cause our joints to behave in ways that we object to.

A new enemy attacks us, anno-domini, and causes our centre of gravity to shift. It pulls everything toward the floor with a mighty force that is hard to resist. It pulls down as hard as we pull up. Crinkles and wrinkles appear in places that were once smooth and firm. The bathroom scales need replacing more often as they are invariably wrong. When we pluck our eyebrows we need a magnifying glass to stop us going mad and ending up bald. Mother nature though, kind as always, looks after us well and makes our eyesight slightly weaker so that when we look in the mirror we cannot see the lines so easily. If we are not careful the once pert behind has turned gradually into a bulbous bum and the inheritance left after bearing our children is in danger of looking like a Buddah belly.

We seem to have shorter nights, or is it just that we have to get up for the loo in the middle of the night more than we used to? Free literature comes through the door advertising insurance policies for the over fifties or whatever. Invitations to attend the launch of new hearing aids are sent to us. Who says we can't hear – we are just more selective in what we choose to let others know we hear. We become more crotchety and speak our mind when perhaps it would be wiser to keep quiet – but why, we ask ourselves? We no longer look for long–term savings accounts because we want to spend the money before we pop our clogs.

The doctor's surgery that we used to drive past now becomes a regular visit on our journey. Instead of talking about the children and their ailments with our friends we now swap symptoms and compare pills. Instead of buying lovely skimpy bras and suspender belts and looking the 'bees knees,' we search for scaffolding jobs that will stop the boulders from reaching the knees. Thick tights now hide the maps of the world appearing on those two appendages called legs and replace the lovely lacy-topped stockings that incurred such ravishing in days of our youth.

We forget when to take the pills we are given and have to rely on a little pack to remind us. We go into a room and come out again because we cannot remember what we went in for. Little things irritate us more. People who take money from us are not sure whether we are eligible for any discount because of our age. Often they look at the colour of our hair and if, like mine, the blonde is turning directly to white, they assume we are ancient. This really annoys me. Of course I do not look that old, but if there is a discount going, well perhaps I will have it all the same.

Quiet carriages on trains are for people like us – well, they are supposed to be. The problem is they are not quiet. After a few moments that stupid frog tune erupts, someone talks loudly and animatedly to their friend and we are all subjected to intimate details of their love lives. I remind them that 'quiet carriage' means no phones. You can imagine the look. A bonus of age, however, is that the experience that comes with it enables you to recognise a mistake when you make it a second time.

Of course it is also a time to move toward well-earned retirement. A time to do everything we never had time for but now find we never have the energy for. A time when we can complete those long walks we dreamed about with our beloved, then rub each other's sore joints and enjoy the experience. Or, as they say, a time to grow old together. Except the government of the day have different ideas and pass all sorts of laws to reduce pension payments or keep us working until we drop into our grave. Make the most of being young, I say, do what you want when you want, do not wait until the time is right because it will never be more right than it is now.

For myself, I am now enjoying being self-employed. I lead school inspections and I absolutely love the job. I have become a true 'social pariah', for no one wants to talk to an inspector. Teachers put up their garlic crosses before my path and members of my own family mumble incantations before I enter their rooms. I can live with this for I now decide when and where I wish to work. I am much more in control of my life than I have been for years.

In this work I share the skills and knowledge I have honed over the years, I listen and I judge. I have the privilege of meeting a different set of people in each school and working with a new group of colleagues on each inspection. We have a lot of fun as well as doing our job professionally. At last I have learned that this life is no dress rehearsal and we should enjoy every minute we are here.

School inspection is a worthwhile process and has helped many schools and teachers make progress. It ensures every school and every teacher is judged using the same criteria and is scrupulously fair. Contrary to general belief, inspectors do understand classroom practice and do acknowledge good work. The hardest part of an inspection for the school is often simply ensuring their documentation is always up to date and meets all statutory requirements. Yes, some teachers are identified as poor within the profession but they are very few, just as there are some poor doctors, dentists, lawyers etc within those professions. In contrast, a great number of inspirational teachers put all their energy and enthusiasm into their teaching and are responsible for encouraging and stimulating pupils of all ages and backgrounds to achieve.

When I began as an inspector, I was taught a very valuable lesson by an extremely competent and experienced retired HMI. As a hard day came to a close and we prepared for a long meeting to discuss our findings, a few team members had not arrived. He simply looked up, made a note of the 'non attendees' on his pad and began the meeting. He knew I was training to lead inspections and after the meeting he told me that I should always begin a meeting at the stated time, even if no one else was present, as otherwise I would never get through the workload and the other inspectors would become lax in their attitude. This advice has served me very well and I begin and end meetings on time, irrespective of how many have arrived. I think it is good advice for every head and manager in the country.

The inspecting process takes me all over the country. I have stayed in more hotels in the last couple of years than in the rest of my life. They are sometimes cold and bleak places for when the bedroom door closes you are alone, you do not sleep because all the noises are different. My colleagues feel the same. However, we all enjoy what we do. It is a pleasure to meet so many bright and eager children and adults and learn about their work, their families, their lives, and their journeys.

Hotels and schools each have their own identities and are intriguing places. Experience has taught me that if I expect the unexpected in both types of institution then I will not be disappointed. On one occasion, in a very smart hotel on the outskirts of Southampton, my colleagues and I were awoken to a great deal of shouting on the floor above. As we listened, it transpired that the wife had just discovered her husband's infidelity. As females we had a lot of sympathy for the woman, but not in the early hours of the morning when we had a difficult and long day ahead of us. After hearing in gory detail exactly what this husband had done, with whom and how, we rang reception who asked the couple to be quiet. (note, we waited until we knew all the gruesome details first). Success, all became quiet. However, the situation was clearly niggling the wife who started up again an hour later, this time throwing the furniture at him. We rang reception again and whatever they did, it worked!

Some hotels have leisure suites but we are usually too busy to use them. After one particularly heavy day a colleague decided to have a swim to help refresh her. When we met over dinner she had us in stitches describing her 'interesting' experience. She and an elderly gentleman were the only two in the pool and as she went into the spa at the side of the pool, he joined her. They chatted politely and then she watched in horror as he clearly enjoyed the effect the spa had on his sexual organs. With undue haste she made a mighty speedy exit to the changing room.

When working in London it is always difficult to find decent, reasonably priced hotels. One autumn morning as we came down for breakfast at a hotel near Ealing Common, we found the restaurant ceiling had fallen in overnight and made a colossal mess. Was this, we wondered, divine judgement on us for criticising the old fashioned reading books about chickens and roofs falling in the day before? We ate our breakfast sheepily in a makeshift room and duly collected our cases but another hitch awaited us. We could not leave via the front entrance as there had been a murder there overnight and the police were conducting a fingertip search. Who says the job is boring?

In a lovely, well-appointed, hotel in a leafy suburb of Portsmouth my colleagues and I chatted amiably as waited for a breakfast table to be cleared. A very slim and pretty young girl walked down and booked a table for two. When a tall, smart gentleman arrived she greeted him warmly but he ignored her and booked a table for one. She shrugged her shoulders then used her mobile phone to ring another gentleman to ask him what he required and for the directions to his house. What a way to earn a living. This hotel was near the port and the airport so a good number of tour guests appeared each day as they began or ended their holidays. We watched and commented on each party with amusement. A coach load of American tourists, some of whom required extra-wide seats and none of whom appeared to understand the word 'diet,' noisily invaded the restaurant and emptied the self-service buffet tables like locusts. German tourists were much less hungry and very polite.

Whilst inspecting a school in a mining village in Washington, County Durham I stayed with my male colleagues in what can only be described as an upmarket transport hotel. None of the rooms were on-suite and all the other guests were big, beefy, heavily tattooed males. Needless to say it had been a male colleague who had booked the accommodation, totally failing to appreciate it was better suited to males than females. Had I been a good few years younger it might have been enjoyable. It is amazing how long a female can hang on when necessary. I got up extremely early to get to the bathroom before all these huge men. The breakfast we were served would have filled three people and the landlady looked at me with utter disdain when I could not eat it all.

Often the service we experience has us in fits of laughter. A lovely country-style hotel in Altrincham turned out to be a cross between 'Acorn Antiques' with a Julie Walter's type waitress and Fawlty Towers, with Basil in the background. On the first morning we arrived for breakfast to find the place deserted. A little, old, doddery waitress appeared and we requested breakfast. 'This early?' was the astonished reply, 'no-one has breakfast this early'. We assured her that we did, so she went to get some tea. The response from the chef in the kitchen when he heard we wanted breakfast was straight out of Fawlty Towers, with the addition of a few choice, but unprintable, words. The waitress brought a pot of tea but could not find the tea strainer. This threw her and we ended up with three huge pots of tea, three tea-strainers, milk, lemon and endless cups. We could have sat there all day drinking tea. As we collected cereal we had to ask for everything and it appeared at her pace – very slow. All performed with a lovely smile, however. By our last day the staff had the message and the tea, toast and cereal appeared at the same time, as soon after seven as they could manage.

It does not seem to matter what the area is like, hotels can still be amusing. For example whilst in Shropshire I stayed in a country hotel with four colleagues. As we pulled into the car-park, three huge 'Chelsea tractors' entered and a number of young male 'county types' spilled out, looking like something out of 'Toad of Toad Hall', resplendent in their brogues, check waistcoats and breeches. Showing off, one of them produced a rifle and was demonstrating this to his friends. One of my colleagues gently walked up to him, bid him good evening and quietly but firmly pointed out that it was illegal to hold a fire-arm in that fashion. The said fire-arm was placed in its box and locked and they swiftly disappeared indoors, tails between legs.

As we gathered for breakfast the following morning, it was clear the hotel did not have many staff. The girl who had been on reception the day before now became the waitress. She was sweet and polite but a useless waitress. The cooked breakfasts arrived on platters that filled the table and left little room for anything else. I must admit I am not into style for the sake of it, especially when it is so impractical. One team member arrived looking a little jaded and complained about being awoken during the night by padding along the corridor. Wondering if it could be a friendly ghost, he apparently decided to investigate. The young waitress had been walking up and down the stairs and along the corridors for her exercise, or at least that was her explanation. We did wonder that, had it been one of the young men who was inquisitive, whether the 'exercise' might have taken on a different complexion.

We try to organise our meals as efficiently as we can when we are staying in hotels, the trouble is that when hotels are leisure, rather than business biased, this is very difficult. On one occasion, we sent our order to the chef during the day with instructions that it was to be served on the dot of seven. It transpired that either he had a different clock to us or he was working on American time. We were duly seated in the dining room at seven and nothing happened. Ten minutes elapsed and we were still sitting on our own. It fell to me to be the ogre and sort things out. This is a lot easier when the staff speak English fluently. I tried to explain that we needed to continue working so must have our meal on time. The look said it all; we must be mad coming to a country hotel and working. Perhaps they were right you know, and we were wrong. I am sure it was a delightful place for a relaxing break. We were the only clients eating that evening and when it came to ordering it ended up as a total farce. Pheasants had not surfaced that week, duck was nowhere to be seen and many other items were 'unavailable'. We persevered for the fun of it and went to bed with barely full stomachs but sides that ached with laughing.

Most schools we inspect are interesting and stimulating places. One, near Ludlow was a pleasure to visit. It was a happy and lively place with friendly staff who took full advantage of our presence. Inspecting is a joy when it works out like this. The pupils were eager, chatty and enjoyed telling us about their school, their pride shining through their conversation. As we left I joked with the team and reminded them to get their work to me speedily so that I could write the final report, and wished them a safe journey home. Two days later one of them, Dermot, was killed in a tragic road accident. I had worked with him often. He was a sound, witty friend whose company everyone enjoyed. I reeled when told the news and felt acutely for his family whom he loved dearly. He was a headmaster. His school lost a guiding light and champion, parents lost a friend and a religious order lost a faithful and loyal supporter and campaigner. He was vociferous for justice, he loved his God and he towered above us all. To think he was just eliminated from this earth in a split second suddenly made me realise how little time we have, all of us, and how stupid we are to fret about things which are so insignificant. I determined to let trivia take care of itself from now on and concentrate only on that I personally felt important to my life. As a consequence I made the decision to cut down my workload and spend more time with my husband and family.

A summer inspection in Liverpool turned out to be a real walk down memory lane for me. The school was in the area we lived in during the 1970's. On my arrival I was certain I had been in the house when it was called 'Lyndhurst'. I sat in the car and polished up the memory cells to see if I could bring back the pictures I wanted. Yes, I remembered that the family who had lived there owned a large department store in Liverpool. They had four daughters who were genteel ladies and never needed to work. However, their father told them that they should not be complacent with their position in society and each daughter was made to choose a charity and support it all her life. The lady I remember chose to work for the blind and supported the cause tirelessly throughout her life, establishing a school and home for the blind in the area. Her family were staunch Quakers. I was amused to see a super, successful, thriving and lively Catholic school with caring children who were incredibly conscious of their responsibility to others, in this house. I am sure the family would have approved. I told the school of the history I could remember as parts of the original façade of the house were still in place. My team were based on the top floor in what had been the nursery and the beautiful central staircase with its glorious stained glass windows was still intact. I was pleased to hear that the City council had placed a moratorium on development in the area to try and preserve more of these beautiful old houses and prevent them from being demolished for faceless, stainless steel, spine chilling flats that all look the same – characterless.

The hotel we stayed in overlooked Sefton Park, a very pleasant location. My room was reached by a journey involving a lift built for Noah and a trek along narrow corridors. It was a dark, dank room with windows overgrown by thick foliage that would not open, no space to work and a feeling of total claustrophobia. I trogged back along the faceless corridor, up Noah's lift and along to the reception. The pleasant receptionist informed me no other room was available. I had my supper with my colleagues and drove the 70 miles home for a good sleep, got up early next morning and drove back. My colleagues were unhappy with their rooms so we had them changed that day. We were given the best rooms after that. My new room was a little like what I imagine a tarts boudoir to be-purple walls, canopied bed and weird ornaments. Perhaps I better apologise to all tarts before I go any further. If that was their best room I feel sorry for those in the worst is all I can say. The one saving grace was the food; it was superb, served promptly and with a smile.

We work in all weathers just like the staff of the schools we inspect. After all, can you imagine the comments if staff managed to get to school in bad weather but the wimps on the inspection team couldn't? When I travel on motorways I leave myself plenty of time for hold-ups, but on my way to a school in Cheadle Hulme I found the traffic coming to a standstill and I was stationary for an hour and a half. I thought there must have been a very nasty accident, so I waited patiently, phoning the school and explaining that I would be late. When I eventually got moving and drove a little further the reason for the hold up became apparent – a flock of sheep had got out of an adjacent field and found their way onto the carriageway.

After I completed my day at this school a few lonely snowflakes began to fall. By the time I reached the airport turn onto the motorway a blizzard had erupted and I could not see more than a few yards in front of me. The snowflakes were beautiful; they were large, fluffy and came speeding from the gloom straight to the windscreen. I would have appreciated them more had I not been driving. Only one lane of the motorway was open. I opened my window and the snow rushed in. An eerie sense of quietness surrounded the car, the tyre noises muffled by the white carpet beneath. I crawled along very gingerly. The car handled well, unlike our Volvo that slipped and slid all over the place in the snow. About twenty miles from home the snow cleared and the road was dry. No one believed me when I told them the conditions I had driven through. I began to wonder if I had imagined it.

One January morning I was due to help with an inspection in the coldest part of Lancashire. I was staying with some friends in Blackburn. This was a real bonus as I had human beings to talk to each evening instead of a hotel wall. It was just as well really in view of the scrape I ended up in. I arrived at the school before 8 am. It was dark, cold and frosty. Real 'brass monkey' weather, if you get my jist. The local streetlights were out because of vandalism and the path was dark. I parked and made my way gingerly along the school path. The next thing I remember was falling sideways over a concrete barrier as my foot connected with sheet ice. I heard a sickly crack and felt a pain like no other in my wrist. I managed to hang on to my computer with my other hand but realised pretty quickly that something was very wrong. I stood up and momentarily wondered whether I was going to fall down again. But we Northern girls are made of tougher stuff than this. I slowly made my way to the school entrance and rang the bell. I walked inside, sat down and calmly asked if someone could take me to the hospital.

Having attended endless first aid courses as a teacher, I knew I had to take off my rings, so I did. As I sat I realised the world was moving around me, literally. School staff were at panic stations, answering telephones etc. Having given them my home number and the number of my friends a senior member of staff drove me to hospital. She drove so carefully I felt every stone in the road, each one more painful than the last. My language had to remain internal as it may not have met Ofsted standards had it been voiced aloud.

I am terrified of hospitals so the panic and the pain were powerful ingredients for FEAR! The nurses and doctors were wonderful. In my heart I realised the situation was grim as I had a soft ball the shape and size of a rounders ball hanging beneath my wrist which did not appear to be connected to anything else. I was sure it shouldn't be there. The staff persuaded me that I needed to be put to sleep so that they could manipulate the bone back into place. They could see my fear, so they had decided to be economical with the truth. What they meant was I had made a damn good job of badly crushing both the main bones in the wrist and they were going to need pinning together in order for them to heal.

I was freezing cold and kept asking for blankets. My friends Wilf and Di, who sat with me, were roasting and peeling off woollies. They had managed to contact Henry, who was conducting a funeral. The undertakers told him I was in hospital so he had to carry on wondering what on earth had happened. As soon as he could, he drove up. I did not want to go into theatre before he arrived. I remember telling the staff that if I died, I wanted to see my husband first. The doctor said his tea break was after my operation and he was desperate for a cuppa, so nothing would go wrong. He could not have said a better thing. The next thing, I remember a nurse asking me to talk to her.

As they wheeled me to the ward I saw Henry along the corridor and burst into tears. We can let go with our loved ones. He sat patiently with me until he thought I was calm and then he went to our friends. I could not sleep. Old ladies were farting noisily and old men were snoring loudly. I was too scared too sleep. I had the indignity of someone helping me to wash in the morning. The embarrassment was intense. I could not use the toilet because it was dirty and I cannot bear dirty toilets. Henry drove me home and I followed up with care locally.

Now anyone who has had a broken wrist and had a huge plaster attached up to the elbow with pins sticking out will know that life gets difficult. The smallest task is a mountain. The limitations cause you to change your fashion sense. Tights are definitely a problem and tracksuits are the order of the day. If you need to wear socks or tights your husband has to help you get them on and all you manage to do is end up on the floor laughing. Why is it that men just cannot get the hang of tights?

The next worse thing is pulling up knickers and fastening bras. This is not easy with one hand, just try it sometime. We had a good few hilarious episodes thanks to that wrist. The physiotherapy for recovery was agony, however I was told that if I persevered there was a good chance of getting almost all movement back, so I jolly well persevered. I was determined to get the wrist working so I did as I was told even though I cried in pain as I did it. The surgeon had been superb and my wrist is almost back to normal. I have much to thank all in the NHS for.

Well, it was back to the grind as soon as the wrist was ready and I could drive. My first inspection after the accident was to a school in Birmingham in the centre of the city. A tough school surrounded by high, spiked fences. Most of the pupils did not speak English. Inside the school was a paradise that stimulated and nurtured all the children and had great expectations of them. As a consequence they achieved superbly with results far higher than national expectations for their age. The children were taught in English then they worked in groups using their own languages and finally answered questions from the teacher in English. The lessons were exciting, the teachers inspirational. We did not want to leave. The children loved school and adored learning. Oh, if only every school could be like that one. The fantastic preparation, the match of work to each child, the care taken to ensure each child had targets relevant to their ability, the vast range of original activities and the utter devotion of the staff to their pupils was stunning.

For the inspection we stayed in a budget hotel by a huge roundabout in the centre of the city. The restaurant was a snack bar and, since the area was dubious to say the least, the three of us ate in the snack bar. As we munched our way through the gourmet cheeseburger and chips one of the team commented on the little squirrel running around outside. As I looked, I realised the little squirrel was in fact a fat rat. I gently mentioned this and the table emptied before my eyes. I told the man on the reception desk and his answer was "don't worry, madam, we don't reserve rooms for them". Well, it takes all sorts.

Do you remember how the press makes a great thing about major events asking questions such as, 'Can you remember where you were when Kennedy was assassinated' etc. So it will be in the future when they talk about Sept 11th. I remember vividly where I was. In a wonderfully happy and lively Catholic school, St Joseph's, in Preston that was surrounded by tall, cold, iron railings with barbed wire around the top. As we talked about our day's findings the head came in and told us two aeroplanes had crashed into the world trade building. We did not believe it at first. Then as it dawned that she meant it, we were all very quiet as the significance of such an act began to sink in. The following day the head mistress led a poignant and incredibly moving assembly at exactly the correct level for the age of the children. That school will be imprinted on my memory forever.

It is always a great pleasure for me to return to the North-east and listen to language as it should be spoken – musically, earthily and with a particular Geordie 'twang'. When inspecting a busy and well organised little school in Blyth I was used as interpreter by my colleagues, all of whom hailed from the South and had great difficulty understanding the children. For example, when one of them asked a child if he could show him where the library was, the reply came back – 'Y, I, haway ower he a' which, being interpreted means, 'Of course I can, come this way please.'

During an inspection in Maidenhead which I was leading, I left a colleague locked in one building and it was not until suppertime that we missed him, poor man. Inspectors are so hard working; he had simply carried on, certain that eventually we would realise what had happened. What faith he had. I didn't like to tell him his fabulous personality had only been missed because of a vacant dinner place.

Occasionally we get to stay in really lovely hotels and it is hard to leave them for work each day. One such on the outskirts of Wolverhampton was shared by a no less illustrious guest than John Prescott. We never saw him personally, but we saw his car and his many minders. They were placed at the bottom of staircases and arrived for breakfast very early. It was fascinating watching the political road show. The minders were there all night too, as I found out when a colleague was ill. He had tried the wild mushrooms for supper and although they had been delicious, they sent his bowel wild overnight. As he knocked at my door in the early hours to see if I had any stomach medicine, I spotted the bodyguards still on duty. So that is how my taxes are used, I thought. Oh, and by the way, I didn't have any stomach medicine and it took the poor man a couple of days to recover from the mushrooms. I now carry a first aid bag full of all kinds of medicines for the team.

Often schools forget to send us maps, so I either rely on internet maps or I use Ordnance survey maps as I love map reading. Nothing is more pleasurable than driving amongst hedges full of wild flowers, watching hawks swooping in the air and listening to Beethoven's Pastoral symphony.

Sometimes a school will leave lasting impressions on us for all kinds of reasons. This happened to me when I was working with a talented team of colleagues who I had known for many years. The school was a totally happy and carefree environment, nestled in the depths of the peaceful Shropshire countryside, surrounded by trees, fields and little else. Our accommodation was in a very pretty farm that had been newly converted to take lodgers. It was so newly converted in fact, that the bedrooms were not complete. The doors were without locks; there were no clocks, televisions or bedside lights. Since we knew each other well no locks was not a problem. On the second evening of our stay I found a pile of four television boxes in my room, a colleague had four aerial boxes in her room but none of us had a working television. The farming clock is different to the daily working clock and the owners had not yet quite adjusted to 'guest time.' None of us were farming people so we had to adjust our clocks to match theirs. He who says the countryside is quiet must be hard of hearing. Animals place their breakfast orders early and birds cheerily welcome the dawn as tired, worn out inspectors are just trying to get to sleep!

We were served breakfast in a rambling but clean farmhouse room containing large and chunky furniture that probably had lived there since the beginning of time. One morning as we tucked into our breakfast, the landlady asked if we minded looking after ourselves as the cow was about to calf. We duly got our own breakfasts and saw the calf soon after it was born. It was a truly delightful experience. The soft, silky animal was snuggled into its mother who appeared immensely proud of her new offspring.

We found strange smells in parts of this school and were told that rats had been discovered below a building. A firm had been brought in and laid poison, when the pupils were not there, to solve the problem. The rats were much cleverer than the pest firm and worked out that if they lay on the heating pipes after being poisoned, their body temperature was raised and they survived. The alternative, when the pupils were not on site, was to 'shoot the rats.'

The beauty of inspections is that we have the privilege of sharing fun with staff and children, of acknowledging the celebration of children's' many achievements, of entering children's lives for an instant of time, of supporting, leading and energising staff and assisting in the continual raising of standards.

I have now watched so many lessons I cannot keep count but I can remember all those inspirational lessons that have left me feeling excited, because I have really 'seen' children learning. The style of teaching is less important than the enthusiasm of the teacher, the interaction between child and teacher, the stimulating challenges presented to the children and the ability of teachers to listen actively and inspire the child. Some teachers ask simple questions that a cat could answer and that do not make children think or use their grey matter. A few teachers do not actually listen to children's answers and give a cursory 'thanks'. The majority of teachers understand and are intrigued by the way each child learns and they adapt their questioning to challenge the individual, stretch the mind and the imagination. I particularly remember a Latin lesson at a boy's school west of London. The room was sparsely furnished and the teacher quite elderly but once he began everyone, including me, was mesmerised. Because he so loved the subject he transformed learning and his pupils held on his every word, eager to know more. We were all disappointed when that lesson ended.

All children do not learn in the same way and super teachers know this. A teacher can teach for 15 minutes. Half of the children will remember what has been said and if the teacher is lucky the same number may understand. What of the rest? First class teachers really listen to all the children, understand how each learns and adapt their approach carefully to each child.

I usually visit schools a couple of times before I arrive with the inspection team. I had planned a visit to a school in the Yorkshire dales in June. Now it usually rains a lot in Yorkshire but when I visited it was one of the hottest days of the year and I felt really sorry for the staff and children. Teachers have to keep going no matter what the temperatures and I sometime wonder if parents appreciate the skill needed to maintain the interest of a class of pupils in temperatures of over eighty degrees. After all, if it was Spain school would end at lunch-time and pupils would return home for siesta. We really must move on with discussing alternative proposals about the timing of the school day in this country, especially if global warming is to affect our summers from now on.

As I walked around the playground at break time a child fell over and a piercing scream cut through the normal shrieks and happy play-time sounds. It was followed by the inevitable long wailing that only little boys seem to make. Looking across it was easy to see the afflicted, a little chap with a very bloody knee. The teacher spotted him immediately and made her way to him. Now in some schools the new code of political correctness dictates that only clinical medication can be applied with sterile gloves. I was so pleased to see in this school that a generous helping of TLC accompanied the efficient and correct application of the correct medication. The tender loving care was immediate and far more powerful than the antiseptic. The little chap went off happily to play and his war-wound was forgotten. It is so sad to see political correctness denying young children the emotional attention they need from their teachers. A comforting arm around a small child when they fall is a powerful medicine and something that the young need. I well remember one head teacher, a Mr X I will call him for obvious reasons, telling me he had decided that 'political correctness' should be shortened to 'pure c★★★'. I said I had not heard him say that!

I always really enjoy inspecting provision for the youngest children. When watching some delightful young children in a large room in a school north of Manchester, I saw one go into the washroom at the side of the classroom. Rather a long time elapsed and the teacher, clearly concerned but not wishing to let me see her concern, was just about to go and check it out when he appeared at the door. His trousers were in a crumpled heap around his ankles and his hands were placed purposefully on his hips. He informed us, in a very authoritative and confident voice, that he was waiting for someone to come and wipe his posterior. He was told gently but firmly that he had to do it himself. I had to turn the other way to hide my smiles.

I find young children to be the most exciting learners. I liken learning to eating as this is a subject everyone seems to understand. Teachers of younger children help them to learn how to eat, how to use different utensils and how to taste different foods and decide upon their responses. They are also careful to make sure children are not allergic to some foods and, if they are, they change them. If children are bored then teachers change the content and delivery of the lesson. The young children thirst for more food and knowledge and the enjoyment they have as they use this is seen in their faces. Teachers of older children, due to the pressure of examinations and tests, only have the time to feed their pupils set food until the pupils are full to overflowing. They then hope they can regurgitate the set food at a given time. So the pupils often suffer from educational bulimia. There is so little time for teachers to feed what they feel is right for pupils of this age that it puts a lot of pupils off the experience.

Recently, whilst watching a nursery lesson, I was very amused to hear the children's comments about different kinds of food, expertly guided by a warm and energetic teacher. One particular little boy clearly loved ice-cream and was holding to the view that it was very good for him. No matter what his teacher said he held to his view and expressed himself with real confidence. Finally he compromised and explained that he had ice-cream for a treat at his grandma's and his grandma would only give him things that were good for him. This was an occasion when the teacher and I both had to laugh.

Each individual child is like a piece of precious jewellery. They have so many different faces and edges. Some of these are smooth and some are rough. Given the right conditions and placed correctly in the light, every edge and face can sparkle and shine like the brightest diamond and light up a room. It is an exciting thing to sit and watch a teacher provide the conditions that enable children to illuminate a room with their learning in this way.

I am always surprised at how classrooms vary. One teacher can thoughtfully and imaginatively produce a stimulating and motivating environment with pupils' work beautifully displayed and labelled, with corners filled by experiments that challenge pupils to explore various areas of their work. The result is a highly motivated class who are immensely proud of their work, their room and their teacher. In another room of exactly the same dimensions a teacher may only have commercial posters pinned up, no special areas, no books and little colour. Now, in which room do you think the pupils are the better learners?

Occasionally I have known an inspector to cause havoc in a lesson, especially when mobile phones are concerned. These instruments are the bane of many a teacher's life and are often rightly confiscated. Once, after the teacher had duly reminded pupils that all mobiles should be turned off during the lesson, the dreaded tone was heard. Surreptitiously, pupils looked at each other with searching faces, knowing that whoever was to blame was in deep, serious trouble. The teacher gave the sort of menacing look that only teachers who are annoyed can give. The noise stopped and the lesson continued. Minutes later it started again. Slowly, quietly and very shame-faced, the inspector rose from his seat, mumbled his abject apologies and left the room. Can you imagine the reaction of the pupils after he left? I expect the teacher's thoughts were rather colourful too!

As I mentioned before, Manchester is a city I visit quite a lot for work. It is large and sprawling and full of people trying to reach their destination, just like those depicted in Lowry's paintings. One November evening, I was with a team staying in a hotel in Bridgewater, very close to a motorway. As we sat down for dinner, we quickly ordered our meal and despaired as each course took an hour to arrive. We were frantic as not only were we famished, we also had much work to complete after eating and could see ourselves working well into the night. On leaving the table, I went to the car park to retrieve a file from the car. By now it was dark, grey and miserable. It was a real November evening when the drizzle cut through your bones like a sharp razor.

I huddled into my cosy jumper as I walked up the aisle to the car. The car park lights were dim so it was difficult to see, however I could not see the car. I knew I was tired and had probably forgotten where I had parked, so I returned to the hotel and asked my colleague, whom I had brought back with me, if he would come and help me find the car. To say I felt stupid was putting it mildly. We both wandered back out into the chill of the night. By now it was 10pm. He could not find the car either. We went to where we thought I had parked and noticed another team member's car had been broken into. Slowly it began to dawn on us – my car had been stolen.

Once the initial paralysing shock had subsided I was in the hotel like a flash, rang the police and they took all the details. All my inspection materials, including the children's work, were in the boot. Of course, there was nothing more I could do, so I had a stiff drink and went to bed. Next morning the police had left a message for me. They had found my car in a rather salubrious area and because it was a high performance car, they had kindly towed it to the police pound immediately. They told me that had they not done so, it would have been stripped bare by the morning.

Before school began I was taken to identify the car and, sure enough, it was mine. As I looked in the boot, however, I realised that none of the inspection materials had been touched. The thieves were clearly not school inspectors. In the circumstances the police allowed me to remove the school material so I could carry on working. However, I also found bottles of brandy and boxes of chocolates had appeared in the boot of the car. They certainly were not mine. The police said the car had been used for a robbery and then dumped. The problem was the thieves had slit all the car seats with a knife, just wanton vandalism really but all needed replacing. The insurance company took control of the car and I did not see it again for six weeks until all the damage was repaired. The nuisance value was immense, but I was very pleased I had the car back as it was my pride and joy.

When returning home from Sheffield quite recently, I stopped on the outskirts of Manchester at a tearoom for a short break. I always try to stop every two hours on long journeys as I find I concentrate better if I do so. I ordered the tea, rang Henry on the mobile to let him know where I was and, twenty minutes later, and went out again. As I reached the car, I thought, 'Gosh, that's funny, I don't remember leaving the window open, and why can I see right through the car and out the other side?' I then noticed that the back windows were also open. Finally, I saw the back seat had been pulled forward. You are probably there before me. Yes, as if in slow motion it dawned, I had been robbed. Thieves had triggered the central locking system, got through into the boot and stolen my laptop and case full of clothes and belongings.

I walked, trembling, back into the café where they let me ring the police. The reaction of the Cheshire police was abysmal. They had no intention of coming out to me, said they would probably never retrieve the goods and the best thing was for them to give me a crime number then I could drive home and contact the insurance company. Bearing in mind that the tearoom had a CCTV camera and there were only a couple of other cars in the car park, it is possible that the police could have seen the culprits if they had wished. However, they did not wish and what could I, an insignificant member of the public who merely contributed to their salary, do? Nothing. I drove home.

My laptop had all the work for the previous year stored on it and all the details of the previous week's inspection. Fortunately I had backed my work up a couple of weeks previously so that helped enormously. A sombre warning to all you laptop owners who carry them around with you, back up your work regularly. Also, all my personal data was on this machine and I was very concerned. I rang the police station again to be told that they would make a note the computer held privileged information – and that was it.

My local police station in Rhyl was very helpful. They gave me a number in London to ring and I was able, for a fee, to sign up with an organisation that makes a record of stolen identity material. It ensures that, should someone try to use the information, they are traced and followed up. So, at least no one can obtain a passport or credit in my name or pretend to be me. However, it still sends shivers down my spine knowing someone knows so much about me.

The fact is, though, life is too short to be scared or dwell on it, so I just got on with it and placed all my data on a new machine sent to me by the insurance company. It was an excellent idea to have insured the machine for use outside the home. All the extra costs paid off for me.

I recently inspected a school in a rough area of Nottingham and felt nothing but great admiration for the staff and head who were battling against the odds to instil a sense of self-respect and confidence in small children who were close to resembling the 'ragamuffins' of the Victorian era. Few children knew how to speak correctly and virtually none had any idea of what table manners were. Outside the school in the estate the law of the jungle applied. The teachers had endless strategies to interest these pupils and give them a sense of responsibility, many of which were extremely effective. Of course the word discipline was high on the agenda and those parents who showed any interest at all supported the strong discipline code in the school. I am not talking about cruel discipline or discipline like that in the tale of the young man who received a parrot as a gift. The parrot had a bad attitude and an even worse vocabulary with every word being rude, obnoxious and laced with profanities. The young man said polite words, played soft music and did anything else he could think of to clean up the bird's vocabulary. Finally, he yelled at the parrot. The parrot yelled back. Then he shook the parrot and the parrot got angrier and ruder. In desperation, he threw up his hands, grabbed the bird and put him in the freezer. For a few minutes the parrot squawked and kicked and screamed. Then suddenly there was total quiet. Fearing that he'd hurt the parrot, the young man quickly opened the door to the freezer. The parrot calmly stepped onto his outstretched arm and said, "I believe I may have offended you with my rude language and actions. I'm sincerely sorry for my inappropriate transgressions and I fully intend to do everything I can to correct my rude and unforgivable behaviour". Stunned at the change in the bird's attitude the young man was about to ask the parrot what had made such a dramatic change in his behaviour when the bird continued, "May I ask what the turkey did?"

I am always kept amused when I look at the work in children's books. In their rush to write down and complete their work they often do not check what they write and this is a constant source of amusement for their teachers. I wish I had kept every 'funny' that I saw over the years. I kept telling myself I would then I would get involved with something else. Some of those I do remember though include the following;

Trees are very good at breaking wind.
The octopus has eight testicles.
My favourite book is the 'Penis and the Carpet'. (The Phoenix and the Carpet)
Oysters' balls are called pearls.
My granddad wets his pants because he is inconvenient.
Dolphins have big assholes in their head to breathe through.
My uncle goes out in his boat with pots and comes back with crabs.
When you go swimming in the sea, it is very cold, and it makes my willy small.

I still go to London occasionally for meetings and now I always dread it. I hardly recognise London any more. Twenty years ago I loved walking along the streets, looking in shop windows and experiencing the excitement of the capital. Now I cannot wait to get out. It is not because of the terrorism scares, for I was often in London at the height of the IRA bombings and learnt to adapt to the difficulties then. No, it is because London is no longer the friendly and comfortably cosmopolitan place it used to be. It is over-crowded, people are discourteous, they push, they shove, they are rude and they are in a perpetual hurry. No-one has any manners. I hate this. My train gets in at Euston and my meetings are in the Barbican area. I usually take taxis now from the station to my destination and chat to the cabbies who happily regale me with all sorts of information. I watch the Londoners scurrying along the hard pavements with their tight faces. They bustle around without looking, they surreptitiously stare at those around them and they seem to lose their tempers at the slightest provocation. In some areas there is a dearth of people over the age of twenty-five. Perhaps this modern city is only for the young – perhaps it was always so.

CHAPTER 10
Flash Gordon

Well, now back to home life. At the beginning of 2003 Henry developed a series of health problems following a serious chest infection. He never regained his former strength, his breathing was more laboured and he became physically exhausted after the smallest effort. Men do not like being ill and they like being unable to do things even less. For almost two years he battled to regain his strength, but to no avail. When he tried going back into the pulpit he was shattered after half a service, so he had to face the inevitable early retirement and this was a very difficult journey to negotiate.

It was found that he had an enlarged heart so he needed to readjust his life to fit the size of his heart. It was interesting to watch the church swing into non-action when one of their employees was taken ill. Apart from the initial get well cards, he received few visitors from the locality over the two years he was sick and very little communication from those in the echelons of power. This did make us wonder about the effectiveness of the caring, pastoral mission of the church. It did not matter, because we came through this together.

It appeared to me that the institution of the church was like an ancient steamroller, clanking and puffing along, trying to make up the road ahead to last a little longer. For those who were on the road and fit to travel things were fine. For those who could not keep up, for whatever reason, the steamroller simply kept on moving, squashing them in its path. Perhaps instead of trying to re-patch the road, the church should be looking for a new and different machine to create a completely new route to God.

By the end of 2004 Henry had no option but to retire early because of poor health. The absolute finality of this was a major blow because, having given a lifetime of service to his work, to be stopped just before the end was a great shame. In over thirty years he had only had a few days off work with ailments such as flu. He gave all his best years to his mistress the church and she took them eagerly, greedily and relentlessly. Now he is left with less than active years and, given half a chance, the church would be asking him to help out voluntarily whenever and wherever but he has refused. Of course he was too young for his state pension so yet again the onus fell upon me to keep us in bread and shoes as his meagre occupational pension was exactly that – meagre. We made the decision to sell the cottage on Anglesey, give the children their share and put our share into a small bungalow in Rhyl.

When I have to go away to work I leave as many meals as I can ready for Henry. His culinary skills have not increased much over the many years we have been together. He can open a tin, boil an egg, grill bacon and cook vegetables 'in a fashion' and that is about it. I have failed miserably in domesticating him. I have always loved cooking and Henry has always loved eating the results, but our waistlines show it. So, no more baking, just diet fodder from now on. How boring this will be. When we were young and dieted the weight went quite speedily but now we are older and diet the weight holds on to the stomach with an iron grip and prising it off is very difficult. Then, when it eventually decides to depart, we find we are left with flesh in places that we do not want it, so we have to find super strong underwear to support in the right as well as the wrong places.

None of my mature friends have found the knack of going to buy underwear in a department store yet. These places are full of young girls with figures that could squeeze through a miniature gap in the fence. Pretty lacy bits and pieces in miniature sizes, some of which would not cover an orange are hanging everywhere. The garments in question certainly would not cover a 'JL' bum, let alone a 'just past' middle aged posterior. Where are the 'builders merchants' garments for goodness sake – the section with the scaffolding, the plastering and the support timbers? They are hidden in the bottom drawers that you can't bend down to or the top rail that you can't reach. I think the svelte young shop assistants take pleasure in seeing us mature ladies squirm as we ask to be shown these items.

Sometimes I wonder if, as we grow older, we are becoming interested in antiques because we are on the way to becoming antiques ourselves. It is interesting that a series of rhyming words are so often applied to the elderly, particularly the female of the species – such as 'sag, bag, and hag.' This is mainly because people briefly look at the outside; they do not take time to look at the inside. If they did, their language would change dramatically.

To keep us occupied in our forthcoming years, we recently gave a home to a crazy but lovable puppy, a Gordon setter, who is growing into an equally crazy but lovable dog. He has become big and beautiful and he 'talks' to us. Any of you with a setter will understand what I mean. He sits at my feet from where he grumbles and grouses at Henry. If I speak to him, he speaks back. Can you tell we are besotted with him? It was not difficult to find him a name. He is a Gordon; we are Gordon's, so he was christened Flash. He does, of course, have a posh kennel club name but he is Flash to us. This is quite appropriate really since all through my career children have given me the nickname 'Flash', though I can honestly say that never once, in thirty-eight years, has such a nickname been used within my earshot!

We have never had a dog like him. He is completely zany and utterly loyal. We could never show him because he cannot stay neat for more than a couple of minutes. I describe him as the canine equivalent of 'Just William'. He is like the little boy who goes into the school gates looking pristine and immaculate and by the time he reaches the classroom door his socks are round his ankles, his shirt-tail is hanging out and his tie is squew-whiff. Well, our dog is just like that. We brush his long feathers and he comes out looking majestic with a shining, glossy coat. If we are remotely near water, he finds it, jumps in and within seconds emerges looking like Pluto from the Walt Disney cartoons.

The cats have the dog totally under their control. The dog, soon after arrival, worked out the order of the family pack. First came the cats, then Henry, then me and finally him. I think he got it about right really. Cats and dogs have a very different view of their 'people.' This is very well illustrated in the story of a conversation between the cat and the dog. The dog said to the cat, 'Do you know, my owners give me everything, they prepare my food, they wash me, they take me for walks, they care for me. They must be God.' The cat replied, 'Well, my owners prepare my food, they nurse me, they take me to the vet if I am ill, they give me a soft bed. I think I must be God.' If you are a cat and dog owner, I think you will agree.

The dog follows us everywhere and is very loving and affectionate. He sits at our feet or lies beside us if we are working. He gives us unconditional love and takes us for long walks every day, when we enjoy each other's company more than we have done for years. As he is maturing he is turning into an excellent guard dog, the problem is he lacks the intelligence sometimes to know when to guard and barks at the wrong people. He is, though, excellent at sensing aggression and often, if passing a large and noisy group of youths, he will growl and bark at them as he can sense the testosterone floating antagonistically in the air. His bark starts in his tail, rumbles slowly along his body gathering pace, finally entering his throat and, by the time it leaves his mouth, a deep and mighty woof erupts. Great for deterring unwelcome guests. On 'Trick or Treat' night a couple of older youths knocked and I could hear their bravado and cheeky comments as I opened the door. Flash hurtled up behind me and woofed loudly. They took one look and ran which was the worst possible thing to do. He chased them along the street and no one else bothered us that night. Good old Flash. I am afraid that he also dislikes Jehovah's witnesses intensely so they no longer visit us – what a shame.

We are so much fitter since he arrived, but he offends our sense of smell regularly. However, he is a good excuse when guests come and a smell is lingering in the house! His certificate for obedience from the Kennel club has to be shown to people to make them believe us.

We have found his presence has the effect of limiting the number of visitors we receive – only those who really like dogs come now. We suspect others make all sorts of unkind comments about him and us and 'lack of control' behind our backs and simply do not come to visit.

Unlike Henry, the dog is particularly fussy about his food. When I was busy working recently, I completely forgot about the tea in the oven. A strong burning smell reminded me and I took out cindered steak. Henry, bless him, ate it happily. However, when he offered Flash a portion the dog wrinkled up his nose at it and walked away. No burned food for him.

We take Flash to the beach each day for a play and this is a wonderful way of meeting other folk, particularly 'doggy' folk. Everyone has a word, a chat about the dog, and comments on what a mess ours looks as he invariably has been in the sea, and you feel really good. The down side is that being a long haired dog, or as a little girl referred to him recently a 'fluffy dog', he carries half the beach back in his paws and his coat and deposits it in the house.

Now we have tried all kinds of solutions to this. We come in the back door and keep him in the kitchen until he dries out. We make him stay in the garden if it is fine, then we find he has attempted to tunnel his way out through what is left of the lawn. We do attempt to give him a shower in the garden on warm days, but we never manage to retreat quickly enough to miss the first massive shake he has afterwards and we all end up soaked. Consequently I now accept the inevitable, dust and vacuum every day and this helps keep me fit.

Being self-employed provides a wonderful sense of freedom. What a joy it is to be able to decide whether or not to get up in the morning, like being a teenager all over again. Then deciding how to fill the day is bliss, no one there to order the day for me and no meetings to attend. Of course, should I be working on an inspection then I do have a set pattern for the day. Also, now Henry has retired from the claws of the church means we can both be ourselves for the first time in years.

One of the wonderful things I can do again now that I am at last wearing my own mask is to laugh and giggle as much as I want. I no longer have to do this on the inside, I can be as free and abandoned as I like with my laughter. A friend we visited recently told Henry that he never realised I had such a wicked sense of humour or that I could be so funny. He said that since I left the church it was as if a genie had been let out of the bottle. That is a good description. Now the genie is free.

I have a group of female friends here, Beti, Jane and Irene who are truly loyal and faithful friends. We are from totally different backgrounds but we know that we are each there for the other should one of us need support. Over the last six years we have met regularly for lunch every month and are by far the noisiest bunch in the restaurant. We laugh a lot, tease a lot, gossip an awful lot, support a lot and bemoan our troubles a lot. When we have finished we feel a whole lot better. Of course, we solve the world's problems when we meet and we could easily be employed to sort out the male population.

We are thinking of writing 'a guide to women' as a manual for men, using the many years experience we all have. For example, we think men really need to understand that when we women say 'fine' at the end of an argument, it is a signal that we are right and they need to be silent. Or, if a man asks us whether he should do something and we say 'go ahead,' it does not mean 'go ahead' at all, rather it means 'we dare you to do it.' Finally if we use the word 'whatever' to a man he should beware, for it is our way of saying '★★★★ YOU.' Lastly, we would advise all men to stick to two simple words that will conclude all arguments and win them endless Brownie points – 'Yes, dear.'

Henry just seemed to be stabilising his health and getting into a pattern of life when wham, that kicking horse appeared again during the summer of 2005. His heart decided to go haywire once more and he felt very unwell. Next thing, he was in hospital for the first time in his life. A very alert and excellent GP diagnosed a problem accurately during a routine surgery appointment and dealt with it immediately. This was excellent service. After he had cared for people who were horizontally challenged in hospital beds all his life, Henry now found himself horizontally challenged.

I never realised how frightening the whole experience of hospitalisation is, not just for the patient but also for the immediate family. We did not know what the future was to be, yet at the same time we were trying to keep everything ticking over, driving to hospital and being chatty etc twice a day, whilst collapsing exhausted at night.

The need to visit Henry was much stronger than my fear of hospitals, so I found my way around the building. I hated the lifts. They were large, cavernous spaces, filled to capacity by people of all shapes and sizes with a whole range of expressions on their faces. Some were nervous and perspiring, some happy and smiling, some upset and drawn. I decided the best thing was to use the stairs, so I climbed up the 80 stairs to the ward each night. By the time I reached the ward, I needed one of the beds.

My first observation was the youth of the nurses and doctors and my second observation was their ultimate patience, kindness and endless supply of smiles. My husband was on a ward with four other gentlemen, one of whom was a little 'wandery' and walked around all night trying to get into other peoples beds, much to their chagrin.

We worked our way through this stay and were so pleased when he was allowed to come home. However, even in hospital he was helping others on the ward, calming them down, listening to their problems. We had trouble making him realise he was in there to get himself better and not to work for others. Just as well he did listen to the other patients though, for although there were supposed to be hospital clergy available no one saw them. It is strange how we make new friends now. A chap in the next bed to Henry in the hospital has become a firm friend. He and his wife live along the coast from us and we have great fun and laughs together. They are lovely people with no church background so they accept us for what we are, not what we were.

When he became ill, I picked up Henry's emails each evening so that I could pass the news on when visiting and keep him in touch with the world. In amongst his many messages was one from an old girl friend. He had caught up with her and a few other old friends to find out what they were doing. In fact, he said he had virtually nothing in common with her, but it was interesting to hear how she had spent her life. Her emails sent much love and kisses and I suspect she was making up for filing him in the 'don't call us' pile all those years ago. She asked for his address to put him on her card list but he did not feel this was appropriate and he has backed off communicating with her. I wonder if her husband knows what she is writing and what he would think of her emails. My friends think she needs a check up from the neck up.

Henry's hospital stay made both of us take stock and was a shock to us both in so many ways. Being in the horizontal position often makes a person think of the vertical. After Henry came home we talked about lots of things and listened to each other more than we had for years. Henry is an Ignatian spiritual counsellor and I am a trained counsellor, but we had forgotten to take time to listen to each other. In retrospect, our long working hours had turned me into a virtual lodger and, to a certain extent, left Henry behind. Henry said it had been very hard to find the 'real' me when I worked all these hours. His hours and the demands that his mistress the church made on him took him further away from his family as time went on. We certainly had grown apart somewhat, as a result of all kinds of circumstances. However we sorted ourselves out and came to the conclusion that we were a couple of old codgers who still loved, enjoyed and really wanted to be with each other. In fact, we often found ourselves in a situation of 'us against the world,' because of our experiences.

Another inheritance Henry mentioned was that, as a child, he was never given affection freely by his mother. She controlled him, as she was a powerful lady. If he ever disagreed he was punished. She blackmailed him often by threatening to leave if he did not do what she wanted. On one occasion she even threatened to put her head in the gas oven. Can you imagine the effect this had on a young boy? It prevented him from trying to talk about certain situations and he tried to avoid conflict of all kinds as much as possible. It helps me understand why he is the way he is and why he never mentioned that he felt we were drifting. His one stand against her was that he would not let her dispose of me-he said he was adamant she would not destroy our relationship as it meant too much to him and, he won.

Over the years I have found that many parents are totally unaware of what they do to their children and of how their actions shape their children's emotional health and personalities. This is particularly so for those involved in bitter and acrimonious separations. I have lost count of the times that I have consoled distressed children who are in tears because their parents hate each other so much they tell each other this within earshot of their children. The innocent children then blame themselves and scar their own lives. As parents, we choose to have the children and should never forget that we are responsible for their future and it is their right to expect us to try our hardest not to scar them.

Of course, I do not condone abuse of any sort either within or outside of marriage but there are ways of protecting children. Far too many times the children in a marriage or partnership are treated similarly to precious china in the list of belongings; because both sides love them and each want them for their own.

This fraught time made me realise that we should not let wounds fester for years; nor should we let work subtly and surreptitiously become our partner or our master to the extent that it pushes out our real partner. Each of us must find the way and the time to communicate effectively and save ourselves pointless pain. All of us benefit from taking the time to rediscover each other. Henry and I have reached a togetherness that comes with long, real, deep and committed love for each other. All we want now is time to enjoy each other. We are very fortunate to have come through the trials and tribulations that marriage, cruelly demanding jobs and many flirtatious women have thrown at us, stronger and still loving each other. I hope my children can have the same length to, and love in, their marriages as we have.

I have two pairs of spectacles now, one plain pair and one with slightly tinted lenses to protect against sunshine. When wearing the plain lenses I know and accept that Henry can, on occasion, be an inherently selfish person who will go his own way at whatever cost to the family or me. However, it is helpful sometimes to wear the tinted lenses to protect against harmful rays. So it is in life, we need to admit and accept we all have our faults, but life is far more bearable if we consider our mugs half full rather than half empty.

We have time now to visit our friends and hear about how they have their retirements time well organised. Many of our friends have taken up hobbies to enable them to keep their own space and identity. We find this strange as we have spent a lifetime being pulled so many ways by so many people, that all we want now is to spend our time together doing things we both enjoy. Ah, well, each to his own.

We have fallen in love with Scandinavia. It is so open and spacious and clean. Whilst in Norway early in 2004 between Henry's bouts of illness we spent a whole morning walking through a lush, green valley. All we heard was the sound of rushing water and songbirds praising the sky, all we smelt were the sweet blossom and berries in the meadows and all we saw was magnificent beauty and grandeur. The effect on our spirits and senses of the majesty of God far surpassed anything cramped into an hour on a Sunday morning. We missed nothing, except perhaps public conveniences.

Of course, once a teacher always a teacher. I was amazed at the provision for primary children in the most outreaching parts of Scandinavia and the excellent play facilities provided for them. Outside a small, timber clad school in an isolated valley near Flam in Northern Norway we found a wonderful adventure playground with imaginative apparatus and safety surfaces. I have often found schools here give too little attention to play. Children's breaks are spent on huge squares of ugly black tarmac that do not promote good social communication and the children return to lessons grumpy and bothered. The very best playground I saw, in Coventry, included a large adventure area, an area with huge floor draughts, chess, noughts and crosses and snakes and ladders for those cerebrally inclined, hop-scotch for those who liked to join in games together, a ball area for the sporty types and a lovely garden area with seats at different heights for friends to sit and chat. Breaks here were really happy occasions, little aggression was to be seen and good relationships were promoted between pupils who were refreshed and ready for lessons when their break ended.

CHAPTER 11

Taking Stock and Moving On

I felt recently that it was time to reassess what I was, what I wanted and how I might achieve it. I think I have been, and perhaps still am, tough and strong professionally but perhaps less so personally and emotionally where I remain shy. I think women generally have a wide range of dimensions all of which differ in colour, strength and impact. No wonder men say they cannot understand us and struggle on trying to interpret what we say and do. I feel that I have managed to wear my different masks well and keep my own mask hidden from all but my family and close friends. I am unafraid to admit to weaknesses as well as strengths. Whilst in St Matthew's School at Yiewsley, the local authority director described me as a 'natural achiever' and in Luton I was referred to as 'the plain speaking blonde from the North'. In other words, a spade to me was a spade and not 'an implement with which to lift soil whilst gardening.' I was privileged to be described as 'intelligent and analytical' by a university professor and as 'knowledgeable and perceptive' by an HMI. It is always encouraging to hear such comments. Of course I am perfectly aware that, over the years, a plethora of less complimentary comments have been made about me.

I do not suffer fools gladly and I have little patience for lazy workers, whether they are teachers or learners. I speak my mind and I have to accept, because everyone tells me, I am a perfectionist. I work tirelessly for success, expect others to do the same and I demand high standards of those who work with me. I am acutely aware these traits can annoy others immensely and drive them mad. I know I can on occasion be an abominable bossy cow and in my professional life I can make others quake. I am still totally passionate about education and getting the best deal for every child, no matter what their needs. I have had to make some very difficult decisions in my career that have affected others. I have always tried my best to be fair and just, mostly I have succeeded but sometimes I have failed. I cannot tolerate injustice. Whilst I have enjoyed each phase of my career and feel blessed to be so fulfilled in my profession, the part that still thrills me most, and the part I know I will miss most when I finally retire, is being in the classroom with the children.

I am intensely proud and fiercely protective of my family and I am thankful for the true and loyal friends I have. I remain lonely, still wondering about my lost family and ancestors. I still find social meetings a pain, even though I have a good number of questions and comments I use to keep me going and have learned to work a room like the best of them. I believe people must take me as they find me, what they see is what they get. I am no longer afraid to be me.

I still love the man I married in the early springtime of my life, although we both now show the signs of autumn. He can always bring me down to earth with one of his hundreds of jokes, even if I now know many of them by heart, and he can always help me to see the funny side of everything. I think I know my own foibles and wrinkles and crevices and try to love them all. If we can manage to believe we are beautiful from the inside out, then others will also see our inner beauty reflected and transformed in our face and actions and we will spellbind them.

Whatever others reaction to me may be I hope my story makes them feel better. Those born before 1960 may understand much of what has happened to me reasonably well. Those born after 1960 are children of the liberated female age, the politically correct jungle and probably feel I should have pulled my finger out and got sorted long ago.

Now as I gallantly stave off the final season of my journey, winter, I hope I have made folk around me laugh and realise that life is a rough old business and it doesn't do any good giving in. We just have to tough it out and keep going. I have encountered many hurdles and, on occasion, mountains and stumbled at them. The secret is to persevere and find the safe route to the top and if one route fails, then simply pick ourselves up and try another. We can all reach the top but in different ways and at different times and what constitutes the top for one person may not be seen as the top for another. In other words, we are the makers of our own salvation. I have discovered that we need to love and believe in ourselves, for if we do not then we cannot let others love and believe in us, and we cannot love others unconditionally. The only person we can totally trust in this world is ourself.

When I look at photographs of myself in my twenties and thirties, I realise how pretty I was and what a good figure I had. Why did I not see it then and where did it go? Probably down the pan with my self-confidence and this was such a waste. I think that, as well as slimming clubs and groups to watch weight, there should be 'soul watchers' organisations to mend, repair and reshape broken souls.

We all have aspirations and ideals in our youth of the 'ideal partner'. The older we get the further away the ideal seems to be and it is always 'just' out of our grasp. We try to make loved ones fit these ideals, when really we should be trying to create new ideals together that make each other shine brighter. Experience has taught me that it is important to learn to love both the nice and the nasty parts of ourselves and our partners, the kindness and the unkindness, the generosity and the selfishness. We cannot change our partners just as they cannot change us. We may be unable to learn to love their warts, so we will have to let them go. If we hang on the ride will be bumpy and the medicine sometimes painful, but we can sometimes find healing and renewal within their love. I have also come to the conclusion that for me although men are from earth and women are from earth, the difference is that women know this fact but men don't.

After long experience, I think marriage is like the weather, some days will be idyllic warm sunshine that envelops us totally, some will be windy and we will get rather thrown around emotionally, and there may be storms that we will have to survive, hide or sail away from. All are normal. However, just like the British weather, each day will be different and, if we hang on, we will eventually have the weather we like. We should not imagine, as the young and naïve do, that love sustains a marriage. It is not that easy. It is marriage that sustains love. That is why the institution of marriage is important, because within it we make serious vows to another person that we hope will last a lifetime, through all the changing temperatures and storms. These vows will support us when times are hard, so that love can survive. The fact is we will all have to compromise in our marriage as in everything else. But then, life is one big compromise is it not? As time passes love, as well as life, changes with age. The initial thrill and passion gives way to a warm happiness simply to be together, wherever that may be and however that may be.

If I was at the beginning of this journey again, I would certainly marry the same man but not if he was entering the same profession. However, after a lifetime in the profession, I do not think he would choose it a second time.

I no longer attend church; I can be free as God is free. For the first time in years I do not grumble about the scales being inefficient or try to persuade myself that the floor is uneven and this is why they are showing drastic figures. Now I can see certain numbers on the scales appear after the dial, not before. This means the diet is working. I am learning to believe it when I am told that I am loved dearly, irrespective of how I look or how I feel, and not to ask questions. Nothing can fill the crevices that have been put there with the worries of a lifetime, I am not gullible enough to believe that creams will make wrinkles disappear and I will never go under the knife. My major treatment will be doing things that make us both happy.

The money that I now earn will be spent. My earthly goods are sorted out and I am beginning to feel as if I have a life again. This must be what they call silver power. I wish it had been blonde power a decade ago, but I must make the most of what is left. I am going to enjoy the time Henry and I have together as much as when we were young, just not so speedily. As Henry says of this new phase of our life–'the best is yet to come.'

We are grabbed by the idea of becoming 'old age' travellers, rambling around the country and perhaps the world in a motor-home. We are going to grow old disgracefully and SKI (spend the kids inheritance) into oblivion, enjoying and maximising every minute of it. Selfish? Yes, well perhaps we are. We have helped our children to set up and be comfortable and happy. We spent our lives serving others, often giving at the expense of our own family and relationship, so now it is 'our' time. I just hope the good Lord allows us the opportunity to enjoy it.

I urge all my friends to make the most of their 'now.' I think that a good dollop of common sense is what most of us need, together with belief in ourselves and also the knowledge that others have been there, survived and come back out again. Plus a few supportive family members together with loyal friends who are willing to sympathise, to be honest, to tell us when we are being a fool and simply to be there when we need them. I have learnt that it is vital to stay close to our 'golden' friends. Like the precious metal itself, their value increases with age. We are very lucky to have many such friends. Two of them, Ray and Liz, we do not see for many months but when we do they are as shiny and as precious as they were when we first met them and it is as if we only parted the day before. As time goes on their value increases and they are the best possible insurance against dark days.

Well now, old habits die hard so they say. So it was with us when we investigated the expense involved in buying a 'shell' or motor home to give it a posh name, for our backs in order to drive off into the blue yonder on our old-age travels.

Henry, in his inimitable male way, would quite simply have gone out and spent all our savings. Me, well as the female of the species I am a tad more cautious. I wanted to know whether I would like being stuck in a small box exploring the great outdoors before I parted with my hard earned cash. I suppose it will be good preparation for being stuck in an even smaller box in the not too distant future, but let's forget about that thought for now. The result of our deliberations was a compromise. We decided to hire a motor home for a week to see how liked this kind of itinerant lifestyle. It cost a pretty penny but it was money well spent. Imagine buying such a thing and then finding out we hated it. Actually there are often vehicles on dealers' forecourts, with only a thousand miles on the clock, for much reduced prices because someone has lived their dream and purchased a motor-home only to discover they detested the life-style. I was determined this was not going to happen to our well-earned cash. We found a hire company on the internet, made enquiries and hired a van. It was not a huge thing, just a discrete van with a tiny toilet, a fridge, sink, cooker and two bench seats that converted into beds.

You would think this was going to be easy for us but the first problem occurred when Henry tried to stand up in the seating area. He was too tall, so inevitably he ended up with a head that felt like the Himalayas after a few days. Every time he wanted to sit down he had to bend over to get into the seat. But when men want something they will put up with anything. It reminded me of our youth. When he wanted an 'early night' he would help with endless tasks just to make sure I had nothing to keep me up! This time, the early night was for another reason – we were plumb tuckered.

Henry had booked us into three different campsites for the week to give us a flavour of the life and a taste of what could be our future. They were all in Yorkshire. The first was near the coast and we arrived in rain that fell in a sheer blanket and enveloped us tightly like a sheet wraps around a baby, soaking us through. Normally we would have stayed in the van until such a downpour stopped, but nothing could be so easy. We had our mad dog with us and he wanted a pee. When he wants a pee he has to have a pee. He stands at the roadside with a smile of utter relief on his face for an interminable time and just lets it go. Oh, to be a dog. So after much discussion, my husband was recruited to do the necessary. He put on a coat and took the dog all of 10 yards, stood aimlessly waiting and getting soaked through until the hound emptied his enormous bladder. The dog was relegated to the front of the van and my husband had to have a change of clothing as he was wet through. However he kept smiling; worried that a grumble would elicit a 'told you so' sort of response from me.

The rain eased a little so I decided to venture out to inspect the 'site' toilets. The word 'site' is very descriptive, because that is exactly what they were – a sight. Not only where were old but spiders hung from the cisterns, the floors were dirty with wet feet and the corrugated roof leaked in numerous places. The smell defied description. Ah well, I thought, we do have the van toilet. Next, I made my way to the showers. They were a trifle better. They looked like something from Mars, funny tubs that you stood in, showered, then came out to stand on disgustingly wet and dirty floors or wooden slats that clearly harboured germs from past centuries. Free verrucas were obviously on offer that week. Showers were definitely off. Good job we were visiting family in the area, we could use their bathrooms.

This was not a good start to our adventure. The blurb about the site said dogs were welcome. They were, as long as they stayed in the van. Signs everywhere said 'dogs not allowed in this area'.

Our first night taught us a few important lessons. I have never before changed into dry clothes in such a confined space as that in this camper van. I soon learnt there is quite a knack to this. You have to agree with your partner on the allocation of a section of floor space that is yours and stay in it while you change. Before you begin, however, you have to lower all the blinds in the van. If these two procedures are not followed, then the whole campsite has a vision of bare old bums banging together as they bend over to step in and out of clothes. Not a pretty sight!

By the time we left this site my husband had demolished part of the garden decorations as he gained experience manoeuvring the width and length of the van around the display, so I think it was 'quid pro quo.'

We drove into a supermarket car park on our way out of the town to replenish stocks and found we were social outcasts. I was beginning to get an inkling of what it must be like to be a gypsy. Motor homes do not fit readily into parking spaces, so we had to go to the far end of the car park and either find a double space that we could fit into or a space that we could overhang safely. This is easy once you know what to look for. We duly stocked up and headed for the wilds of the Cleveland hills. The next site was in the middle of nowhere near a beautiful little village. It was a gem of a site. We were met by lovely people who could not have been more helpful. When they knew it was out first experience, they were only too pleased to help in any way possible.

Henry drove us onto our pitch and hooked us up to the electricity. Before that we filled up with water. Those of you who are old hands at this game will know that filling up with water entails attaching one end of a hose to the tap on site and placing the other end in the water tank of the van. This is easy when you know how. On the first attempt of course all kinds of problems rear their ugly heads. For example, the hose will not attach as you have the wrong connection. Then, when some kind person has come to your assistance you realise that you cannot see the tank and have to rely on hearing to tell you when it is nearly full. What do you think happens if someone is hard of hearing? Correct – wet trousers in a very embarrassing place and a wife dissolving with laughter that drew even more attention to the predicament.

This place was very 'doggy' friendly as long as the dogs were tethered, which is fair enough. So, Flash was duly tethered outside the van and he settled down happily, watching all the comings and goings like a little old woman behind her net curtains. Being in the country we had the company of masses of rabbits who were very inquisitive and came up to the van door to peer at the strange creatures within. They did not like Flash much though, as he had other ideas for their welfare, namely for them to provide him with a nice tasty snack between meals. When they realised he was tethered we watched them play games with him. They smiled at him and teased him, encouraged him to strain as far as he could, then scampered away and showed him a white tail. Who says animals do not have a sense of humour?

We soon realised that this style of van did not suit us. In order to make the bed each evening we had to open the rear doors and this was a pain. Also, it occurred to us that if it was raining bed-making could be a very soggy job. We were lucky that the weather stayed fine. We had to climb up a step into bed and it was a hoot. My husband could not stretch out as he is 6'2" and the bed was 6.' He had to curl up the remaining 2 inches as comfortably as he could. He has never been a tidy sleeper and thrashes about wildly during the night, so I was left to sleep on a tiny section of the bed! Of course if he needed the loo in the night he had to wake me up to climb across me, then climb back over me into bed. Not a good idea.

Another item soon appeared on our shopping list – doggy charcoal biscuits. In our spacious home the dog could be sent out of the room or into the garden whenever he created a disgusting smell. In the van there was nowhere to send him except to the corner furthest away from us. So we found some charcoal biscuits and persuaded him to eat as many as possible so that we did not have to find gas masks for ourselves.

We did not need to use the tiny hand shower in the van because the site had immaculate shower facilities. In fact, they were much cleaner and better appointed than the bathrooms of many hotels I have stayed in. It amused me to see children of all ages paraded off to the showers each evening. Some trotted along quite happily and others were almost dragged by their ears to get washed. I watched with interest the antics of the children on the site. Children of differing ages played well together, not needing television or computers to have a good time; instead they made up their own games and were physically exhausted when it was bed-time.

We decided that we would to do some walking along the Cleveland Way whilst staying here and it was a super experience. The dog scampered free along the path and we sauntered behind, happily enjoying the fragrant air and the blissful silence that surrounded us. The inquisitive sheep, which poked their noses around the trees to investigate the strangers appearing in their territory, were duly amused by the long haired creature. The dog was, of course, on his lead when the sheep were in the vicinity. Although we are convinced he would not hurt them, like all dogs he is curious and if they ran from him he would follow his instinct to chase. This can be disastrous for sheep as they can break limbs or have heart attacks from the shock and the farmer has every right to shoot the creature that is worrying them. After all this is their territory not ours so we must obey the countryside code. We strayed a little from the main path and found a real jewel awaiting us.

At the top of a narrow, steep lane on the crest of an escarpment and in the midst of an established copse of oak, beech and sycamore trees was a beautiful, small and very old Benedictine priory. It was open and on entering we suddenly found ourselves within a serene and calm place that enveloped the body as well as the soul. It was a simple but dignified place, immaculately clean and well ordered with some information about its history and an invitation to all who entered to become part of the spirit of the place. Brothers from the order walked from the neighbouring village each morning to light the candles that flickered peacefully and gently, throwing a golden mysterious glow around the silence that pervaded the building. The sense of continuity built up over the years from the prayers and reflections of pilgrims surrounded and permeated the whole building. It seemed to hold body and spirit in a tranquil and deep peace and we sat and simply absorbed the atmosphere.

Outside was equally as peaceful except for the manic dog beavering around, smelling all the tree stumps to get the daily news and to discover what other four or two legged creatures had visited recently. We sat in the pleasant clearing enjoying the pine-scented air as he gathered all the information he needed. He returned from his jaunt with soaking wet feathers and looking nothing like the majestic hound he was supposed to be, instead he was a bedraggled mess.

On returning to the village we visited the church that was also part of the Benedictine presence in the area. Although it was early afternoon the church was open to all. Again, on entering it had a strangely beautiful calmness. What a pity it is that such places cannot be left open in cities where their sense of awe, wonder and quiet support are needed by so many people. Sadly an underclass of vandals find such places an easy target for their aggression therefore, understandably, everyone is denied access.

Feeling totally invigorated in body and spirit, we returned to the site to make tea and spend an enjoyable evening sitting reading in the fading sunshine. To be totally free of traffic, television, telephones and work is a rare treat. All my life I have loved reading and found I could escape quite easily in a book, so it was a joy to be able to do this again. Everyday life can so easily trap us into systems that we do not like, that are not good for us and that, slowly and surreptitiously, break down our souls. If only we had the confidence to stand up and ignore such systems and be ourselves more often I am sure there would be far less depression.

The following morning the experience of the walk was still with us, but in a different way. You see, in our hearts and minds we are still young and fit however in reality we are beginning to dry up and leak in places that we were not aware existed until now. Unfortunately, we do not take proper account of the wrinkles and creaks that seem to have appeared quietly and sneakily over the years. The result is that when we got up we staggered in a robotic fashion rather then walked, as our muscles had seized up in the most unusual places and bones we had forgotten about required oiling as they squeaked and screeched at us. So, slowly and somewhat gingerly we trotted down for a shower and prepared breakfast. The dog of course does not suffer from such problems, he arose fully fit and up for another invigorating day.

I never knew how many folk of assorted shapes, sizes, dispositions and backgrounds enjoyed camping. As we tidied up, a couple of well spoken and quietly established middle-age cyclists pulled up on the patch next to us. Now it was clear from their pigtails and clobber that they had probably done their 'time' in the hippy era. We tried to guess what they did. Henry was certain they were teachers. Why did he reach this decision? Well, because they had a definite method for unpacking, they bossed each other around, they 'looked' like art or design technology or classics teachers, they were meticulous in the way they erected their miniature igloo tent and their gear was a good country green. Funny how he has such preconceptions of teachers and yet neither I nor the many members of his family who are teachers fit his image-or at least I do not think we do. Perhaps I am wearing my rose-tinted spectacles again.

The couple were polite and pleasant enough folk and exchanged the time of day when they passed. They retired early that night as there was little else for them to do when darkness fell, climbing into their miniature tent one after the other and zipping themselves in for a very pleasant evening. At least I presume it was pleasant from the bouncing of the tent. When inside a tent, many folk seem oblivious to the fact that those outside can see movements and hear noises.

I soon realised that the camping clock is governed by the sun and the moon. So, soon after daylight, our neighbours arose. We were better off as we were more comfortable and could lie in if we wished, so we simply watched them as they emerged. We had quite a good window blind that stopped others watching us but enabled us to see them. Now I realise that camping is not 'The Ritz', but what we saw quite took our breath away, together with Henry's eyeballs. The lady emerged first, wrapped in a sensible and warm fleecy jacket that ended at her hips. That was it really, there appeared to be no other clothing apparent to the casual onlooker or nosey parkers such as us. We think she had knickers on, but she was extra large and such garments must have been extra small because they hid nothing and left nothing to the imagination. When she bent down to retrieve something from her bag I had to lean over to catch Henry's eyes before they fell to the floor and rolled away. She may, of course, have been wearing a thong, one of those disgusting skinny things that cover nothing, get stuck in unmentionable creases and are definitely only for those without the Lopez style buttocks that are becoming fashionable. Henry hadn't seen a sight like that since reading girlie magazines. After a while she re-emerged from the tent with a towel and went for a wash. I could see a lot of male eyes following the sight – who says men do not like bigger ladies? Mind you I think that, like us, they were probably intrigued to see if she was or was not wearing knickers. Henry's only comment was rather restrained really. When he saw the aforementioned lady bending over he simply commented that her husband didn't need a cycle rack for his bike.

Later in the day, after Henry had fully recovered from such a rude awakening, we walked to a pretty, small and very well-kept village nearby for a newspaper and were confronted with something out of the Victorian era. At first we could not find the newsagents. On a corner as we walked we spotted a tiny village shop that doubled as a post office and seemed to stock anything and everything and, if they didn't have what you wanted they would try to get it for you. We progressed further through the village we passed a little tea shop from which emanated the gorgeous smell of home cooking. An old table and even older chairs were placed outside with, alongside, a bowl of water for dogs. So we decided this was to be a definite visit for later in the day.

The village square itself was very pretty, with flowers in tubs cascading over the pavements and attractive stone cottages boasting colourful gardens that lifted the heart. Two neat and flower bedecked pubs faced each other and a well-stocked outdoor shop indicated the area catered well for the needs of walkers and ramblers.

But still we could see no sign of a newsagent. So the obvious thing to do was to ask, which we did. A group of locals were only too pleased to help. We were directed to a derelict looking shop front and an unforgettable experience was about to unfold. We had actually walked past this once thinking that it was empty and probably up for sale – how wrong we were.

I stood outside holding the dog whilst Henry trotted into the shop. He had trouble opening the stiff and ramshackle door and at one point was worried he might demolish it. As he stepped inside he stepped back into the 19th century. Old brown wooden counters lapped around all sides and an even older lady stood behind them. Each wall was covered in brown wooden shelves from floor to ceiling, most of which were empty. A few dismal packets of sweets and crisps were laid out haphazardly on the main counter. The atmosphere and smell of the years pervaded everything, including the ancient shopkeeper. She was small and alert with straggly white hair that had no particular style. Her eyes were sharp and her teeth worn away with the years. 'Careful of the floor', she croaked. Looking down Henry realised why the warning was needed. In the middle of the floor was a gaping hole with jagged floorboards around it. No notices, you were just expected to avoid it. The words health and safety had not reached this old lady. Quite refreshing really, as these words have become the excuse for not allowing so many everyday, normal things to happen. Children can no longer play with conkers in school playgrounds because of 'health and safety'. For goodness sake, surely conkers are better than violent computer games? Children cannot climb trees because of 'health and safety'. If these words had been prevalent in the time of our greatest explorers half the world would never have been discovered. Let's get some sane perspective on this for goodness sake. Well, tirade over, we'll get back to the shop.

I think Henry was mesmerised for a few minutes as the scene took him back to his earliest childhood days. He was brought back to the present by the reedy little voice asking, 'Yes?', then again but louder, 'Yes? He asked for a newspaper and was told to rummage through the pile on the floor by the back counter. This was self-service of a different kind. He stepped over the hole in the floor, looked through the pile of newspapers and found the one he wanted. He was amazed to discover that all the newspapers were that days, he was expecting to see them dated 1940. When he paid, the old lady brought a battered margarine tub that doubled as a till onto the counter and carefully counted his change. She was sharp as a nail when it came to the money. The tin was full of money-coins and notes all stuffed together. It was returned to its little hidey hole under the counter when she finished. The look on her face said 'What are you waiting for now-scarper!' So he did.

He was literally speechless when he emerged. We could see the locals laughing at our astonishment. Such an experience was, whilst amusing, also very refreshing. It is rare to see someone and something so untouched by the modern world and all its 'so-called' glamour and glitz.

Our last site was outside Harrogate, a very refined and genteel town. The site was packed as it was school holidays and this helped us decide that, if we had a van, we would travel primarily out of school holidays. Having spent a lifetime with children I want to be far away from them in retirement. I do like children; I just do not like to hear them whining and whingeing at their parents and observing the lack of control exercised by parents whilst I am trying to relax. It amazes me that parents ask a child to do something, the child refuses, the parents asks again, the child refuses again so the parent gives up.

Watching the antics of parents on this site I was also aware of what bad examples many are to their children. They sit around in the evening smoking then take young children into bar lounges and expose them to the sights and smells of adult drinking. No wonder a generation of children grow up smoking and drinking from an early age, are unable to communicate with each other or with adults and then are blamed for their 'laddish culture'. Parents need to look a little nearer home before laying all the blame at their children's feet. All was not lost however as a good number of younger fathers were to be seen playing games on the fields and chattering happily with their children whilst mothers were preparing picnics. These children were the most contented and well behaved because their day was geared to their needs, they were important and equal and not just appendages to their parents' bad habits

I am amazed at the lack of embarrassment folk have about how they look first thing in the morning. In many ways I envy them and I hope I learn to be less self-conscious as time goes on. As a new day dawned on this site with the sun shining and promise of a warmer time ahead, the ladies emerged from tents and vans to trot along to the showers. Some looked as if they had suffered a rough time the night before, others walked in their sleep and no-one made any effort to look glam. What a refreshing change. I am sorry to disillusion young men who have visions of their pin-ups emerging from sleep pristine and gorgeous, but what we saw was how people really are first thing in the morning.

Well it was time to return the van to the hire company. It had been a successful experiment. If we had hated the experience it would just have cost us the week's hire charge and we would not have gone ahead with a major purchase and wasted a considerable amount of money. We also learned that we needed a van with a bigger bathroom, one with sufficient space for Henry to stand up in, with a bed he could fit into and one with a rear lounge as we liked sitting looking out of the window in comfort. We decided we did not want a van with a back door as this involved far too much fiddling around. So, the decision to buy was made and we put our list together. The search then began in earnest.

CHAPTER 12

Choosing Our Motor Home

Now Henry is hopeless at haggling. We have a friend who is a brilliant haggler and works on the assumption that prices are just guides. No matter what he is buying he will try to get it cheaper. He is certainly not poor; he just enjoys bartering and wants the best possible offer. We have been amazed at how many times prices have been reduced for him. Whether this is because he is elderly, or the assistants are just galled by his cheek or they just want to get him out of the shop I do not know.

When we were in Russia at a street market Henry looked totally non-plussed when stall holders tried to haggle with him. This was quite useful as it extricated us from the constant pressure to buy. I cannot ever remember him haggling for anything in this country or abroad; he just pays what is asked. Since his heart problems he is even worse than before, if that is possible. So whenever money is mentioned he sort of disappears into the background and, even though he is 6'2", he manages to become invisible. When this happens I simply have to get in there, get on with it and sort things out. So I had fully prepared myself for the inevitable, 'Are you buying or selling?' techniques, and the 'We only have this one model left and it will be gone quickly, so you will have to make up your mind' and the 'I really cannot let it go any cheaper otherwise I will be losing money myself'. We heard them all and my answer to every one was the same-rubbish. If they wanted a sale I knew they would come down to the price we wanted to pay and if they did not then there were plenty of other dealers selling the same make that would.

We visited many showrooms and stepped in and out of so many motor-homes I could not remember which was which. It is incredible how many shapes and sizes they come in and how ingeniously they are fitted out inside. In fact, every make had beautiful models in their ranges. Our decision was to purchase one with sleeping accommodation for two only as this is to be 'our' time and 'our' life. We knew exactly what we did and did not want in such a vehicle and made a list of these things, so whenever we spotted something on the 'no' list in a van we simply left it and looked at the next. It is very easy to be swayed by the magnificence of some vans and forget what you are really looking for, so the list was very useful.

We got beds out and put them back to make sure we could handle them easily. This is important for old age travellers as the constant lifting and pulling required in some vans can play havoc with the muscles. We played with high level and low level cupboards to make sure we could both reach them without me needing to stand on stools all the time, or get down on hands and knees. It is very useful being two different heights. My husband reaches the high cupboards with no problem at all and I reach the low ones – good planning that. We even sat on loos. The latter was quite vital as, if you have a big behind, you do not want to have it squashed and nipped as you try to squeeze it onto a minute seat. The salesmen do not mention this of course.

When confronted with the inevitable aggressive salesmen I simply eliminated them with a good old 'school marm' glare as I knew we could get the vans from many outlets, so really they did themselves no favours. Many of the larger dealers are very helpful and do not mind if you explain that you are just looking in order to get as much information as you can before making a decision. Often they will answer all your questions and just tell you to have a good look at their stock. It can be quite tiring driving around the dealers, especially if, like us, you live in part of the country where there are very few and it is quite a drive just to reach one.

We were just about fed up when we realised we were by Teesside airport and a large company, Cleveland motor-homes, was based there. Our brother-in-law spoke highly of them so we thought we may as well call in. There were masses of new and used vans to look at. After welcoming us the salespeople simply left us to get on with it and suggested that we come and ask if we needed help or wanted keys to access vans. What a difference this made. We pottered for ages. We stood up in vans, sat down in vans, we made up beds and laid on them, we sat in the lounges and put our feet up. We sat on the loos and turned around in the showers.

Just as we were about to leave we spotted a van on the forecourt, an Autosleeper Rienza, that we had not looked in so we asked for the keys. As soon as we stepped in we knew it was the one for us. It had everything we were looking for and it just felt 'right'. However, it was more than we were prepared to pay. We began some negotiations but were unable to reach a deal with the salesman so we gave our details to the firm and left quite deflated. The firm rang us a couple of weeks later to ask if we were still interested. Following further haggling we agreed a price suitable for us and it was ours. It is a good idea to look for a van in the late summer before the following year's models come onto the forecourt because the dealers are keen to clear space for the new vans and are more malleable when it comes to negotiating deals.

Organising the journey across to Teesside to pick it up seemed to take ages and we were like two children waiting for Christmas morning and a new toy. However we filled in the time with a catalogue of accidents and began to wonder if we would actually make it to the collection date. We were driving along the sea-front one morning, when Henry overtook a van that was crawling along at ten miles an hour. As we overtook, the van driver decided to turn right without looking into his mirror and simply banged into our side, pushing us across the road. We hit the opposite kerb and this bounced us back. Fortunately there was no other traffic, which was the reason my husband had judged it safe to overtake in the first place. It was a very nasty feeling, simply watching this idiot drive into my side of the car and being totally helpless to stop him. I automatically squeezed myself away from the door, dreading the worst. Henry is a gold medal ROSPA driver and his skill saved us from a nasty crash. However even wearing a seat belt I was flung from side to side and then forwards again before we stopped. Henry got control of the car quickly and managed to stop. I thought he was going to have a heart attack because he was so furious with this idiot in the van. The language that erupted was a remnant of his days in marine engineering rather than his time in the church.

A young man got out of the van and pleaded with us not to report the accident as there was no damage. He was obviously blind, as all our tyres were shredded and the side of our car was damaged from one end to the other. He was in a sorry state as he thought he might lose his job, he was also upset because Henry shouted at him. Now I am usually calm and I was very patient but I really felt hard pushed to be sympathetic to the fool who had just caused the crash and made such a mess of our car. I rang the police to report the accident but the young man left before they arrived. Not before I had taken his details, however, and the name of his company. The police came very swiftly and were extremely helpful-but so young. I thought of all the youngsters I had taught who had entered the force. I was benefiting from their skill now. The garage arranged to collect the car for repair the following week. Henry had a minor attack of irregular heart beats from the shock and had to take it easy for a few days. Being thrown around left me with a sore and stiff neck for weeks and it took months to go. This is the problem with age; it slows everything down, including the healing process.

Whilst waiting for 'V' day (van day) to arrive, not only did we have a car crash but Henry had a visit to casualty. As we waited for the garage truck to come and pick up the car and tow it away to be repaired Henry was looking for something in the loft. He had not been in the loft for almost a year and, in that time, we had upgraded the house. Almost all our carpets had been replaced by wooden flooring. We found, to his cost, that this made a difference to the stability of the ladder. There should be a warning to all older men that they have to take conditions such as flooring into account when climbing ladders, as they are no longer as agile as in their youth.

He was in the loft and I was reading in the lounge. From the lounge I can see along the hallway and the loft entrance was in my view. I heard a screeching noise and looked up. To my horror I saw the ladder opening up and falling in a horizontal fashion to the floor. As if this was not bad enough I saw Henry follow it, at first in a vertical position and then, as his foot caught in a rung of the ladder, horizontal as he was thrown backwards. This whole process was accompanied by, at first, expletives and then moaning. It was like slow motion although it happened in a split second.

I ran through and found him breathless and groaning as the fall backwards had clearly winded him and he was in pain. My school first-aid training kicked in and I asked him not to move while I looked him over. But, you know, men of a certain age do not do what they are told. Or perhaps that should be men of any age do not do as they are told, or have I just been landed with a particularly awkward example of the species? He wanted to get off the ladder as it was so obviously uncomfortable, so I put my hand under his head and he edged off the actual ladder and lay half into the study and half in the hallway. I could not see any limbs a peculiar shape but knew that, even so, he should not be moved. Now the study is the only room in the house that we left carpeted and, of course, the carpet is new and a pale beige colour. As I gingerly put his head on a towel I realised my hand was covered in blood. I looked more closely at his head and could see it was a mess and was clearly a casualty job. Being practical, I told him not to bleed on the new study carpet, got the phone and came back to place one hand firmly on the towel to try to stem the bleeding. With the other hand I called the ambulance.

What a farce this was. I got through to the emergency services and I gave the requested details. Then, after asking me for details of the accident the person on the phone suggested I put something on his head. I explained that I had done so. I was then asked if we had children or pets in the house and I explained we had a dog, a Setter. 'Oh', said the lady, 'can you move him outside or lock him in another room please?'(she clearly knew what buffoons Setters are). Now, bearing in mind I had a phone in one hand and a head in the other this was not going to be an easy manoeuvre. I know women are particularly good at multi-tasking, unlike men who can only do one job such as falling out of the loft, at once, but this request even had me flummoxed. She then suggested I open the door ready for the ambulance. So, I thought, I have to hold the towel on the patients head, lock up the dog and open the front door. Ah well, I had no choice but to let go of the head, lock up the door and open the dog. Or was that the other way round? I was by this time in a panic as you have probably noticed. As I opened the door I saw the pick-up truck arrive for the car and I felt like screaming. The ambulance then appeared and, at the same time, a good friend appeared. This latter appearance was as if a prayer had been answered. After all, why did he suddenly decide to call by? Apparently he was driving in town and just thought we might like a call – how right he was.

The ambulance men took one look at Henry and decided it was casualty for him. They then took a second look and groaned – he is 6'2' and a good 16 stone. I admired their courage as they strapped him into a head brace and stretcher and carried him to the ambulance. As they did this I sorted out the garage men and they removed the car. I then locked up the house and the dog and our friend took me to hospital.

We cannot speak highly enough of our local general hospital. By the time I got there Henry had been x-rayed, examined and treatment prescribed. No bones were broken but he had damaged the soft tissue in the shoulder, his spine had been traumatised and the swelling and bruising was beginning to show. At 64 years of age these were no mean injuries. His head wound was so jagged they had to stick it together with glue as it could not be stitched. Rather like 'Humpty Dumpty' really.

After the doctors were certain no bones were broken and he would repair better at home I was allowed to bring him home-gingerly. A few days later, he had the imprint of every rung of the ladder on his back in various hues of blue and purple. When our friends kept asking if his fall was caused because he missed his step, his answer has been – 'no, I hit every one'. He could not move his shoulder for a while and this took months to heal, much longer than a break. The shock of the fall, in addition to the bump in the car, had really upset the rhythm of his heart and he had to have a few appointments to get this back to normal. All in all, it took a good six months for him to recover and almost a year for him to get back to where he was health wise before the fall and the car crash.

Now, what were we going to do about the van? Well, for men the collection of a new toy is a bit like sex – if they want it bad enough nothing will put them off. So it was with the van. We had a hired car, courtesy of the insurance company, whilst our car was being repaired. So I drove us to Newcastle, returned the hire car and our brother-in law drove us to the showroom for the van. It was pristine and had the lovely smell of new upholstery and sparkling wood polish. Henry had taken strong pain killers and convinced everyone he could drive perfectly well. He did drive perfectly well, but not without pain. I had never intended to drive such a huge contraption but I had no choice. So we stopped off at a site in Knaresborough for a night to recover our senses and I took over this 24' monster – all five feet of me.

The secret of driving such a vehicle is remembering the length and the fact that it takes longer to do everything, including stopping, otherwise the width is similar to a car and the need for driving care is much the same. I say that quite nonchalantly now but I admit my first time at the wheel was totally hair-raising for me, and more so for Henry who decided the pain he experienced when falling was nothing to the fear he experienced when watching me drive.

A most amazing thing happens when you sit in the motor-home, put the key in the engine and set off. The troubles and pace of the life outside simply dissolve into nothingness and a surreal sense of peace and tranquillity overcome you. Your body relaxes and shrugs off the tiresome push and shove of modern living. It is as if you have entered your own little womb again and you are in total control of the direction, speed and level of travel. Time is no longer working against you but with you. You are no longer fitting too much into too little; instead you learn to make the day fit whatever you wish. It is a feeling of freedom that rarely is allowed to surface during a hard-working life and it is to be savoured and enjoyed. It is the nearest thing that we have found, on land, to luxury cruising at sea. If we get stuck in traffic we really don't care. If we take a long time to make a journey it doesn't matter. If we fancy a cuppa we stop and make one. If one of us is really tired we just go and have a snooze while the other drives. Bliss.

What I have found most amusing of all is the reaction of other drivers when they see a white haired woman 'of a certain age' driving this monstrosity. Most look once, then stare and point at me as they comment to their wives that is shouldn't be allowed. Of course they are just envious because they are not driving it. It is clear that in their view women are incapable of being in charge of such a vehicle. It is only my good upbringing that prevents me waving at them with one or two fingers. Younger folk in particular are clearly miffed that oldies can afford such a van. The problem is that it is not until you are older and have spent a life-time working that you can afford it. We once had a chap stop when we were parked up and comment that the van must have cost a pretty penny. It was said very sarcastically, so the reply was said sufficiently coldly to send him to 'brass monkey' land if you get my meaning.

The really great thing about the van is the view from the cab. I now know why lorry driving must be great fun – you can see everything over hedges and over garden walls. The countryside takes on a whole new vista and once boring roads become interesting because you can now see the bigger picture. When in towns and in traffic it is easy to look into front windows and great fun to peek and see what is going on. In the countryside we can now see over the hedges and spot all kinds of wildlife, transforming the journey. Roads that we have travelled on many times take on a whole new perspective.

Anyway, here we were, back home and ready to begin a whole new experience together, as oldies. The first thing we are getting used to is the length of the van, especially when parking. We have decided to have reversing sensors fitted and the sooner the better. Each time we need to park I have to go behind the van and guide it in. I am getting better at this. At first I stood in the wrong place so I could not be seen in the mirrors. This elicited all sorts of comments from the cab – most of them unprintable – but I soon got the hang of it. The only time Henry guided me into a parking space I got out discovering I was a fraction of an inch from hitting a huge tree branch. When I pointed this out his comment was – 'Oh, I didn't look up, I only looked at the kerb!' I think the situation may have been somewhat different if I made such a mistake.

We could not wait to have our first real adventure in the van so we joined the Caravan club and the Caravan and Camping club. This is because folk advised us that these organisations have good, safe and secure sites that can be trusted to have agreed standards of cleanliness. The facilities on site are good and everything is to hand. They are also monitored by helpful wardens and most are quiet and very well cared for. So, we booked ourselves into a site on the outskirts of one of our favourite places – Cambridge.

We are learning that stopping for a break in the van is very different to stopping in a car. We need to use two parking spaces if we stop in a normal car park. On motorways the secret is to use the caravan or coach designated bays, and, if they are full, the lorry bays. This gives much more room and more manoeuvring space. If we decide to pull in on the roadside we look for lay-bys that are far back from the road and separated from it with hatching or fencing. This is because the draught from lorries can make the van rock from side to side a little, which is unnerving if we are sitting on the loo or have a cup of tea in our hand.

If we are travelling through a town or skirting around the outskirts then a large supermarket is a really good place to pull in for a reasonable stay. We get two hours free in almost all large supermarket car parks and can usually find a double space furthest away from the entrance. Should we not wish to use the van facilities, then have toilets and cheap cafes are to hand in the supermarket.

The site at Cherry Hinton in Cambridge is a lovely site in what was once a quarry. The pitches are on different levels and there is lots of greenery and wild life around. A dog walk is nearby and five minutes walk away is a fabulous park with masses of grass, wonderful old trees and a lake. Everything a dog and his people could possibly want. Further down the road is a lovely fish and chip shop that does really good sausages, which are the dog's favourites (we are on a diet).

As Cambridge has a special place in our hearts it seemed appropriate to begin a new chapter in life from this place. We decided to walk along 'memory lane' and find the little terraced house we rented. It was so small that if we rushed in too fast through the front door we found ourselves in the back yard before we stopped. We looked in estate agents windows and, when we saw the extortionate sums these little houses were fetching now, passers by had to catch our eyes as they jumped out of their sockets.

Our little house had been demolished after we left to make the entrance to the adjoining dairy bigger but over the years the dairy had closed, the land was bought by builders and the two houses that were demolished had been rebuilt. We then walked to the school at which I began my teaching career. It was still there, but with many extensions. It was good to know that, almost forty years on, our happiness could still be captured in a simple walk along old familiar paths.

We walked further along the road and made for Parker's Piece, a large expanse of grass with criss-crossed paths that lead to different areas of the City. When I taught in Cambridge, once a week I would bring the junior girls to the 'Piece' for their sport, as we did not have a field at the school. It was rather embarrassing as all the male students would gawp at these well-made eleven year olds in their shorts, running around and playing rounders. Ah, happy days. Walking in the centre of Cambridge we realised there was no way we could bring the van into the city as every car park had height barriers. Some of our favourite shops and little nooks and crannies had disappeared in a conglomeration of 'improvements' to the shopping experience. We shall see!

The bus stop to the city is quite near the camp site in Cambridge and the buses run often, so there is no difficulty in getting into the city. It is important to be canny with your money however. On our first bus trip the conductor persuaded us to buy day tickets, even though we just wanted one journey into the city and one out. On our second journey we were wiser and simply bought a return ticket, saving ourselves £2 each. It is many, many years since we used buses so this was a steep learning curve. I think the bus drivers probably fill more churches than the clergy, for their driving puts the fear of God into all their passengers. We hung on to the poles in the aisles as we sat because the drivers fling the vehicles around. I realised why there are bells at various intervals down the bus – this is so passengers can press them and they do not have to get up until the bus stops, thus saving themselves the indignity of falling into the laps of other passengers.

We decided to try out the swimming pool one day. On entering the building we realised there were no exceptions for senior citizens there, as in Wales. It was full price. We did wonder how any elderly person who existed on a state pension managed to swim and keep fit, as the entry fee was rather high. After all what is the point of the government pushing a fitness campaign for the elderly if the elderly cannot afford to get access to the places that will keep them fit. Anyway, I digress. We chose an 'adults only' time as, being a nervous swimmer, I hate being jumped on by unruly kids, and we went in. Henry is a strong swimmer and he simply ploughs through any pesky little rascals who deliberately get in his way and he usually ends up with a clear lane so I follow on behind. This was a very pleasant, airy and well-organised pool in the city centre, but the changing facilities were nothing to write home about, considering the entry fee. When we got into the pool we found it was not adults only at all. I swam along and watched the antics of a gay couple as they argued over the jewellery one partner wore. It was interesting listening to their camp words and petulant expressions.

I embarrassed Henry mercilessly when we were ready to leave, so much so that he went to sit down in the café and pretended not to be with me. You see, I went to the desk and demanded our money back. The assistant was about to get awkward, so I put the old headmistress hat on. It always works you know, the imperious holier than thou tone and the well-practised glare, especially when I know I am right. I argued that we had been misinformed, the session was not for adults only and our swim had been ruined and curtailed. We got our money back, so we had enjoyed a free swim.

We had been blessed with really hot days that reminded us of the summers we spent in Cambridge all those years ago, riding our bikes along the Backs and having great fun just being together. The little terrace house we lived in had a quiet and enclosed back-yard, or 'courtyard' as it would now be called, and was an absolute sun-trap that lent itself well to nude sunbathing. Of course in those days, good muscles held everything in the right place so the figure was really good and proud to be shown off. Nowadays the shape is still the same but the overhangs are bigger, the muscles lesser and pieces are ready to fall off so nude sunbathing is definitely out.

We had great fun just being together even if we couldn't get up to all the things we used to get up to then. Following the super weather came the inevitable storm-our first in the van. As dusk approached, the sky turned blacker and blacker and the rumbling of thunder grew louder and louder. The dog began his wimp routine and he hid underneath the chair. We do not encourage this; he manages it all on his own.

The first drops of rain dried as they fell, the ground was so hot. Then the drops became bigger and more persistent until the incessant pattering turned into a loud banging on the roof. I had chosen to go and have a shower just before the rain began and I truly did not hear it when I was in the shower, as I was listening to the radio. When I emerged and stepped out of the door of the shower block, I stepped in again immediately. The paths had become raging torrents as the water flowed down the site. I could hardly see the van as the rain was just like a sheet of water.

I waited until there was a slight lull in the rain, covered my head with the towel and made a run for it. I took off my shoes and just waded through the water. It was a great feeling really, a bit like being a child again. Children experience things with such freedom and it's good if occasionally we can revert to such a state. By the time I got to the van however, it was as if I had never had a shower. My legs were splattered with grass and mud, my hair was dishevelled and I was drenched through. Henry took one look and simply laughed. It was great to get back into the van and it reminded me of when I was a little girl watching the rain from my bedroom window and being all cosy inside. We had everything we wanted in the van and the pattering of the rain on the roof gave us a feeling of great security.

I must tell you that our dog has developed a distinct taste in people. One evening as we walked back to the site in the dark a couple passed us and spoke to us in a friendly manner, mainly asking about the dog. They were a very pleasant couple, rather older than most hippies but of a similar ilk. The lady reminded us of Marina from 'Last of the Summer Wine', with her skimpy shorts, high heels, dyed hair and rather thick make-up. The chap had three-quarter length trousers and legs that resembled a map of the world. In fact I don't think any part of him was not tattooed. Our dog looked hard at them and then gave them an almighty woofing. It was extremely embarrassing and all we could do was apologise. We will have to extend the dog's appreciation of fashion.

Since our visit to Cambridge I have found it is very useful to find the web-site of the city we are visiting and research information about car-parks and general facilities such as supermarkets and bus stops and routes before we set off. Contrary to the view of the young, we oldies are pretty good on the internet and find our way around well, if just a tad slower than those with a few less years than us under their belts. Often, the listed car park sites do not mention whether or not they have height barriers, so I simply email the transport department at the local council, tell them the size of the motor-home and ask what facilities there are in the area for parking. This saves a great deal of grief on arrival. I have found that most local authorities are extremely helpful and give plenty of useful information if I just ask.

On the way home from Cambridge we stopped to see Ray and Liz, two of our golden friends, in Hemel Hempstead. The new estate we lived on thirty years ago was now well-established. The young trees were tall and strong, but as we walked along the street where we lived the memories were fresh and vivid. As I looked at the window of what had been Christopher's bedroom, the years rolled away and I remembered bringing him home from hospital to that room. I saw the path where Naomi tripped on her skates and broke her leg and it was if I could hear her screaming. So many memories, where can the years have gone? It was as if we had never been away. Except for the fact that the wide open spaces in the area had been taken over for housing, the streets on the estate were clogged up with cars, the circular road was covered in speed bumps and the ribbon of housing between Hemel Hempstead and Redbourn was growing with frightening speed, leaving few fields for children to enjoy. Also, although none of us would admit to it the facial lines had deepened, the waistlines had thickened and the aches worsened but the spirits were as alive and vibrant as ever. In our minds we were the same age as last time we saw each other. God is very thoughtful as he reduces the effectiveness of our eyesight as the years advance so we cannot see all these glitches.

Because summer journeying had begun late for us, the summer was over quickly and we then had to think about what our autumn journeys would be. Travelling out of school holidays is a luxury for me. It is one of the things I appreciate most since retiring. During autumn there is a dearth of children on sites. Now, don't get me wrong, I do love children, but now that I have reached this time of life I also appreciate a bit of peace and quiet. In our naivety we enquired of a certain camping organisation if they had 'adult only' sites. Their reply had us in fits of laughter. It was very carefully worded as they clearly thought we were weirdo's looking for some kind of sex haven.

Since it was quite a while since we had seen Henry's family, most of who live in the North-East, we decided to visit a place we had frequented in our youth – Whitley Bay. Forty years ago we often came to the lighthouse on a sunny summer evening on Henry's motor-bike and we have many fond memories of the place. This is why we chose a site overlooking the island. It was idyllic. We opened the curtains each morning to the sight of small fishing boats collecting their lobster pots and the lighthouse shining brilliantly against the rising sun. We walked the dog along the cliff tops and felt the same searing North wind that we remembered from our youth. It had not eased in all those years. By evening we slept soundly.

The beaches in the North-East are spacious, sandy, clean and usually empty – due to the winds. On the Eastern side of the country beaches experience good size waves that crash against the shore making a distinctive 'shussing' sound as they drain away. If you are brave enough you can have a paddle in the sea but I warn you that you will come out looking like a biro refill. The dog, of course, is totally oblivious to the cold and hurtles full pelt into the sea, then lies on the beach. He ends up carrying loads of sand on his coat and is expelled from the van until he dries and shakes off the sand. Wet dogs and new vans do not go well together. The North-East is well known to us and we took the opportunity to visit places we loved such as Bamburgh with its magnificent castle towering above the beach and the village and Lindisfarne with its history of spirituality going back to St. Cuthbert. We had to cross the Causeway to reach Lindisfarne and, of course, we read the tide tables first to ensure we did not get stranded. The causeway is quite long and, believe it or not, someone in a new motor-home got stuck halfway along recently as the tide encircled him. He waited in one of the special emergency towers on the causeway but watched his beloved motor-home float away. What a silly waste.

We soon found out it takes a little research to discover sites that remain open during the autumn and winter. We found a fabulous site in Pembrey nature reserve that remained open until late in the year so off we went. We have discovered that, as we travel, it is great to pop in and see friends and family all over the country and we can keep in touch with everyone much more so than ever before. On the way we managed to visit friends and catch up with family news and enjoy ourselves. For those of you who have never visited Wales you will not really comprehend the different pace of life and traffic here. You need to take a deep breath before your journey and slow down so that you are not too far ahead of the locals.

Pembrey is a quiet site in the midst of an extensive nature park in expansive dunes on the South Wales coast. It is possible to walk straight from the site, through the national park, to a magnificent beach that allows dogs. The walk is through pine woods, dunes and grassland that is beautifully cared for and very attractive. Our dog, Flash, thought he was in heaven. He is now three years old, but being a Gordon Setter, he thinks he is still three months old. We are learning that setters all seem to share this trait. His brain cell (notice the singular here) is on time share with another dog and the other dog seems to have it most of the time.

On our first morning there we set off through the park early for a long walk and it was absolutely beautiful. Tall pine trees were covered with frosty spiders' webs whose intricate patterns glittered in the sunlight, and the sharp aroma of pine that seeped into our frozen nostrils was uplifting. We had a ball with us because it is the dog's favourite toy. He cannot be separated from it. If we want to ensure he will behave when we are out we simply leave his ball in the hall and he stares at it all the time we are out. It exhausts him so much that, by the time we return, he does not need a walk since the mental energy involved watching the ball drains him. Whoever said dogs are intelligent needs to think again where setters are concerned.

Anyway, I must not digress. As we walked he ran through the forest at full pelt. I suppose to the unknowing the dog can look quite fierce as he is a good size and his black colour can be rather forbidding. However he is no hound of the Baskervilles, rather the hound of the basket cases, I am afraid. We threw his ball as we walked and he chased it and brought it back – such an easy game for us. We had purchased what we nickname 'the hurly stick'. This is a long stick with a holder on the end for the ball. You use it to throw the ball a really good way. It is far easier than using arms and shoulders that are in a certain state of wear and tear due to the ravages of age.

As Henry threw it along a forest path the dog raced after it. Unfortunately the dog only had his eye 'on the ball' so to speak and did not notice a wooden post in his way. He careered into the post, head first, and ended up in a heap on the floor. This was straight out of a Disney cartoon, except the birds fluttering around his head were immediately joined by the pound signs floating around ours as we envisaged a trip to the vet. We hurried over to him, by which time he was sitting up, his eyes not totally focussed and wondering what the hell had happened to him. He tried to get up and collapsed in a heap. So a little TLC was required. We gently stroked him until he could get up and walk. The rest of the walk was cancelled and we returned to the van. We got the name of a local vet just in case we needed it, but the dog laid low for the rest of the day with an enormous bump on his head. Our hope was that it may have knocked some sense into him. The next morning he was back to his old self, bumps forgotten. How I wish we could have such resilience. If we fall, the aches begin a day later and seem to creep right through the body until they leave via the toes or fingertips.

Obviously dogs need to relieve themselves before bedtime so we always have to have a walk before bedtime. This is good really because it gives us some fresh air and helps us sleep too. As we walked through the park and the site we heard much shuffling as creatures of the night began to emerge. Bats and owls were awakening to begin their patrols. The most exceptional sighting we had was of a badger, which trundled across the grass to investigate the area. We stood absolutely still as we had never been so close to a live badger before. He pottered around and then obviously smelled us and shuffled back into the woods. What a joy that was. Each morning a range of birds visited the trees surrounding the van. A very cheeky Robin was a regular, but many types of finches also visited expecting tit-bits. As we ate our tea one day we spotted the 'site fox', an extremely brazen chap who investigated every van to see if any scraps were available. Although we did not have children with us, we did admit it was a great place to bring children to observe wild-life at first-hand.

There was just time for us to fit in a visit to mid-Wales, which we love, so we chose a site inland from Aberystwyth. We really should have known that blurb which declared 'a short journey from the sea' did, in fact, mean quite a few miles with no hope of public transport anywhere in the vicinity. Always be aware that in Wales even when there is public transport, unless you are in a good-size town it usually means a bus arrives twice a day on Tuesday and Saturday. The site was in a small and picturesque valley, with only sheep and cows for company. This was fine but it meant the dog had to be kept on a lead all the time and he did not take too kindly to this. The site was quite empty so we pulled onto a row with only a couple more inhabitants – one motorhome and a caravan. The folk were, as always, very friendly. Darkness came early and with it came the beautiful clear and silent, black Welsh night.

As morning dawned, we saw one of our neighbours trot off early to the shower block. A while later she returned to the caravan, waved to us and shared a few friendly words about the weather. She then came out to her car, her bag and duvet in hand and loaded up the car. The chap with her helped. Then, after a good clinch and kiss off she drove. It was all very happy and amicable. We thought very little about it really.

After a super day travelling along the Welsh coast we returned and bedded down for the night. As darkness drew in a car pulled up by our neighbouring caravan. Out stepped a very presentable lady, bag and duvet in hand. She was warmly greeted by the same gentleman who had bid farewell to another liaison that morning and into the van she went. The next morning the same pattern emerged. We were intrigued. This chap had a very interesting lifestyle – but we were only booked in for two nights so could not count how many other unsuspecting females were to visit him during the week.

We needed a few very minor tweaks to the van as we bedded it in so we organised a journey back to the dealer. We decided to book in at Stockton on a site adjacent to the white-water course on the Tees. As we approached we wondered what we had done as industrial sky-scapes loomed into view, with massive cranes and machinery surrounding everything. However, we ploughed on and found ourselves in a little corner of beauty hidden amongst this sea of black and noise. An area of industrial wasteland had been redesigned and designated as an area of special scientific interest. It was a sparkling jewel with herons nesting, seals in the River Tees and all types of sea birds making their presence felt.

We have learnt to trust the caravan organisations, as their sites are high quality and very well placed. There was sufficient space for the dog to play and walk, so he too was happy.

As we awoke each morning we pulled back the blinds to see a sharp white frost on the ground and covering the trees. It looked cold but we were snug as ever. I watched a few rabbits brave their paws in the frost and try to nibble the grass when suddenly a large hawk swooped down and struck one of the rabbits a fatal blow. I was very surprised, but not half as surprised as the poor rabbit.

The dog is as lively in autumn and winter as he is in summer. However, the grass is not as dry and the ground not as firm. I can tell this because his paws have suddenly grown in size – they are now half paw and half mud. Fortunately he is a good dog and quite happy to have his feet washed – this is helpful because he would otherwise be spending his time outside shivering. I am fast turning into a van proud person.

Like many others we have worked solidly throughout our lives and been quite successful. We have saved hard, set up our children and really enjoyed the pleasure of purchasing our new 'home'. It was quite sad for us to hear comments emanating from some folk linked to Henry's past profession about our ability to buy our van. Perhaps they should be thinking more about the sacrifices he gave up to work wholeheartedly for them instead of being critical now that he has nothing to do with them.

Winter came without us realising it and fewer sites were open. We found that the Edinburgh site is open all year round so we decided to have a trip there. The last time we visited Edinburgh was to see the Tattoo almost 40 years ago. The site was lovely. It is just back from the banks of the Forth and on a main bus route into the city. It is possible to go for long walks along the Forth or to visit the city and all its sites. If you have a dog it might be useful to bear in mind that the pitches nearest the main road can be quite noisy with buses and traffic so if your dog does not like traffic you are best finding a pitch away from the road. The bus stop to the city is right outside the gate of the site and for a small sum you get into the centre. Edinburgh is a stately clean city, with wide pavements that make walking a pleasure and the shops are great too. We had forgotten how forbidding the castle is, imposing its presence over the city. We had also forgotten what a steep climb it is to reach the castle. The inevitable kilted pipers were piping away all over the city which was quite pleasant really. We trogged up the Royal Mile as this was the gentlest approach to the castle and we walked back to Princes Street Gardens using the twisting path down from the castle. This is murder on the knees and, we decided, only for the young.

We journeyed to St Andrew's the next day and found a parking site alongside the beach that was ideal for motor vans with plenty of space and within an easy walk of the attractive town. St. Andrew's is an elegant and dignified town. It is spacious, clean and polite and greets visitors with courtesy. For the bookish there are many book shops and for the fashion conscious the shops are different and original. If you love to eat then the bakers are wonderful. In fact there is something for everyone with taste and decorum.

When our sojourn in Edinburgh was at an end, we drove home through the border country. Here we found lots of good size lay-bys that had been positioned to give maximum benefit of the stunning views of heather-clad moors that looked wild and bleak as the first chills of winter began to creep over them. Occasional farmhouses appeared and we wondered how the inhabitants managed in such unforgiving countryside.

In many ways the seasons do not matter in a van, you can travel when you want. We just look at the weather map of the UK, see where it is going to be sunny and go, but in the winter there are few sites open and even fewer that welcome dogs, so we are quite limited in where we can stay. It is years since we visited the Lakes so we decided to 'test the temperature' so to speak and have a weekend there. We booked into a pleasant enough site near Grange-over-Sands. It is the first time we have visited this town and it could possibly be the last. The name is a misnomer to begin with. What sands? If you have a pair of binoculars you can just about see some yellow sand in the far distance, past the grimy, dirty, evil looking quick sand and mud that has seeped its way to the foreshore. Notices are everywhere warning you of the dangers of the area. In the twilight the area takes on a sinister feel and the cold, grey mist envelops you as it quietly and surreptitiously creeps its way closer to the shore.

We spotted a signpost that pointed to the promenade so off we went. We negotiated a steep hill, a railway crossing and some steps to see this wonderful sight. It was a pleasant walk along a stretch of concrete paving with the eerie silt and green sludge on one side. Even the dog was cheesed off. Having seen this 'non-sight' we then had to negotiate our way back, this time climbing up the hill. As I said, it was twilight by this time and the day had been absolutely glorious. It had proved to be a crisp February day, with a brilliant, clear blue sky. However, as the sun set the cold wound its way into the air like a slithery snake. Not just cold – bitter cold. It sort of anaesthetised us as we walked. First our faces froze, then our mouths seemed to make odd noises as we tried to form words, finally our bladders froze. Now that takes some doing at our age.

We reached the high street and saw a sign for 'shopping'. Ah, we thought, there's bound to be a cafe where we can warm up. Well, we walked to the end of the street, which took only a few minutes. It seemed to us to be the sort of street where we would not be surprised to see shops with bi-focal windows, grocers displaying cans of large print alphabet soup and pubs advertising draught Sanatogen! This was an elegant, genteel town for gentlefolk of a great age. To describe it as 'a cemetery with lights' would probably be too unkind and give it a false sense of activity, but I bet that's what any young folk would think of it. The shops open late and close early, which probably reflects the lifestyle of their clientele.

We found a café at the end of the street. It looked as if it would be lovely, if the confectioner's window was anything to go by, with fabulous home-made fare adorning all corners. Guess what, the café was closed so we carried on walking back to the van and had a wonderful cup of tea there. It felt as if we had been to the dentists as our mouths and faces slowly defrosted. We have renamed it 'Grunge over no Sands'. I can just imagine all those who live there having kittens when reading this but I have to say it as I saw it. We sorted ourselves out for the night back at the site and snuggled up warm to watch TV. We decided we would try the bed as the large double it is supposed to be instead of the two singles we had been using. It was great – we slept the best sleep yet. It felt wonderful to be really warm and safe and to listen to the wild wind and the rustling trees all around. Like being a little child again. What more could we want from life – we were free, warm and, as Henry said, utterly contented.

Our second day was spent pottering around the lakes. We parked in a fabulous place alongside Lake Windermere and were the only ones there. As we opened the van door, out Flash jumped and played for ages chasing the ball. We did nothing except throw it and he ran like mad. Rather sad really, how can we say he is intelligent? Putting him on his lead, we then walked around the lakeside. The beautiful sunshine on the lake was rather like a crown of sapphires sparkling through a lacy diamond pattern and certainly uplifted the spirits. The path around Lake Windermere is, on occasion, right next to the waterside and the rippling sounds together with the quiet stillness are mesmerising. I imagine it can be rather hectic in the high season though as it is so pretty.

Windermere is well served for parking, both in the town and around the lake and all the possible amenities you could wish for are within walking distance and the park and ride facilities are good.

We left Windermere refreshed and made our way to Ambleside. Now I had been to Ambleside as a child and remembered a photograph of me at the lakeside standing on a rock. It has changed little. A café had replaced the old tea-hut and a posh landing stage replaced the rickety affair that we used in the 1950's, but the smells and the view and the boats remain. A wonderful car park at the lakeside had fabulous views and motor-homes could park there easily.

The dog, as usual, brought us down to earth again. His paws were caked in mud. Now we are not house proud but there was no way this mud covered mut was coming into our pride and joy. He was tethered up outside and we filled a bowl with water. He is such a good-natured beastie, he happily allowed us to wash his paws in turn. So much mud for four paws! It took three bowls of water to remove the thick brown gunge. Then his paws were dried with kitchen paper to clean in-between his toes. His prize was a charcoal biscuit.

Because we want to go to Norway with the van Henry is trying to get plenty of practice driving on narrow roads. The Lake District is fine for this. I must say, though, he was very thoughtful to others and pulled in often to let folk pass. He remembers the many times we have cursed as we sat behind a caravan or motor home for miles. As we drove around Consiton water the road became narrower and narrower and, as I looked down at my side, all I could see was a rather big drop to the lake. Ah, I thought! When another vehicle came towards us I held my breath and thanked God I was not driving as I think I might have had a minor fit.

Coniston Water is more isolated and rugged than Windermere. It has a lonely haunting beauty in places and is not visitor friendly. Of course there are places to park but they are not well signposted and you are usually past them before you spot a small finger post pointing to a picnic area or parking area. If you are travelling this way do look very carefully. If you pass the sign there are no turning points and usually the next place to stop is miles away and toilets were pretty non-existent on this road. The van impressed us with the way it handled hills and inclines efficiently.

Believe it or not, in the middle of nowhere we passed the inevitable golf course. We have a dislike of golf courses. They take up masses of room in beautiful places and deny the general public access to vast swathes of land. Long ago when men and women gathered outside the villages and towns, cursed, walked around and beat the ground with sticks it was labelled witchcraft, now it is called golf. Of course if the wretched things have to be there then they must be unisex. Not, as the age old story goes, **G**entlemen **o**nly, **l**adies **f**orbidden!

If we do not take care of the van everything dries up or leaks – like getting old really. I have noticed how skin becomes thinner and rather flaky if left alone as we grow old. Like soil, skin needs watering, but there is no need to spend a fortune on special ingredients as many of the cheaper creams do the job just as well. I have also noticed that hair has a habit of thinning on top. It leaves your head and finds its way to your chin and above your lip and I have recently discovered that none of my friends travel anywhere without a pair of sharp tweezers in their bags. We are very odd creatures we females. Now what I am going to say may sound drastic, but if you simply rinse your hair with plain water and do not use any lotions, potions, colours, shampoos etc for a month at least, it is almost certain that your hair will thicken and look so much better. The tough part is doing it. Simply do not tell anyone and see what they say. I guarantee you will not smell and will look a lot better.

At most camp sites a rather strange phenomenon is to be seen – men washing dishes. Yes, I did say men washing dishes, and usually of their own accord without any prompting. It seems to be the done thing. At some point of the day the men walk to the dishwashing sinks and do all the dishes. Some of these men would never consider doing this at home. They stand for ages and chat to each other and return to the van with masses of gossip for their wives. It seems to be a male version of 'over the garden fence'. I am sure that Les Dawson got some of his scripts from these conversations.

We decided to make a winter visit to Cambridge. This time, our rose-coloured spectacles were misted up with the intensely cold winds and bitter dampness that pervade and infiltrate the fen country in the winter. We had forgotten about the bone-crunching cold that reaches the parts nothing else can touch, but we were soon to be reminded of it again. I am sure that even the local brass monkeys were frozen solid each morning. Henry wanted a piece of computer equipment and knew there was a particular shop somewhere in the town that sold such an item. So we bussed ourselves into the town and began the walk to the shop. After all these years I should have known better than to trust his sense of directions. An hour and a half and extremely sore feet, freezing fingers and a numb nose later we arrived at the blessed shop. Memories of the area had kept us going. It was a good job they had the required item otherwise my patience may have been tried just a trifle too much. On the return journey to the town I was running short of nostalgia so I directed us back, which cut the walking time down by at least half.

It felt cold enough for snow and the sky was a stark grey colour. Sure enough, we had a dusting of the white stuff. Of course, the children in the area were thrilled and bounded straight into the parks to pick up the frozen droplets and form iridescent sculptures that sparkled like diamonds when bathed in the narrowest shaft of sunlight. Their bright, happy faces and shrieks of delight showed they were immune to the temperature of the flakes. It was a pleasure to watch their unadulterated joy. The kids were making slides then taking running leaps, slipping and sliding along and, more often than not falling head over heels and loving it. They shrieked as they gradually became soaking wet, soggy and happy. I loved snow when I was teaching. I used to enjoy taking young children outside and simply letting them feel the snow on their faces, in their hands and on their tongues. Children's reactions are so natural and unassuming, if only we adults could retain the joy and innocence of childhood when we meet new experiences. Our cynicism taints us as we grow older and so often detracts from our natural responses to the beauty of nature.

The dog also had a fun time with the snowflakes. At first, he stepped on the white carpet with some trepidation as he had never seen anything like this before. Then, as he realised it was firm, he padded around and tasted it. He looked up at us with a black face and white nose. Soon he was racing around and trying to catch the snowballs we threw. He was most disappointed when the game was over.

Forty years on from our first life in Cambridge the situation in the park as the snow fell was, however, rather different for us. Except for making snowballs for the dog, we were avoiding touching the white stuff at all cost. When older fingers make contact with snow they freeze rapidly and the slow and painful defrosting process takes hours. We were also extremely cautious of our footfalls as we walked. Sliding for us would be a very unhappy experience, most likely ending up in a casualty unit with a different kind of hard white stuff all over.

A very pleasant site at Southport remains open all winter and this was our next destination. This site is very near the town centre, within walking distance, so it is useful for shopping. It is also very close to the beach and this is great for the dog. In fact, one day we drove down the coast a couple of miles to Ainsdale and parked on the beach, opened the van door and simply let the dog go. He had a whale of a time. Southport is a pleasant town with many good quality shops. It has masses of attractive gardens with lots of seats and shelters should it rain. The town has wide pavements and we noticed a good number of elderly folk zooming around on their buggies. We will remember this for the future.

We have learnt that good winter sites book up early. This was the case when we decided to go to York and had to take a cancellation. I was not surprised as the site was super. It was on the banks of the Ouse within walking distance of the city centre and next to a lovely park that had been donated to the city by the Rowntree Foundation. York is a beautiful city that manages to encompass old and new without spoiling either. The historical features are accessible and superbly maintained and the parades of shops are well stocked. We had great fun in the Castle museum discovering the wonderful Victorian street, recreated using original artefacts collected from throughout the area. As we approached we looked through a gallery depicting the early to mid twentieth century and found ourselves staring at items that were familiar to us such as poss-tubs, wringers, gas washing machines, black lead fires and ovens. A box of toys on the table in which were jacks, marbles, a skipping rope and a spinning top could have been mine. In fact, as we heard a party of children approach, I told Henry we better move fast as they would think we belonged to the collection of artefacts!

CHAPTER 13

The Big 'Six-Oh'

In my youth the age of majority was 21. I could not vote until that age nor could I get married, without parental permission, until I was 21. It was frustrating and having been away at College I found such rules absurd for I could earn my keep and live alone but not make my own decisions. Then the age of majority became 18, which seemed a far more sensible proposition. Now the age of majority appears to be whatever you want it to be. It is said that forty is the new thirty, fifty is the new forty and sixty is the new fifty. So guess what folks, I was fifty this year. Who am I kidding? Not you anyway.

I am a 'baby boomer', a child of post-war Britain, so it has been my privilege (ha) to become sixty this year and enter the era of 'old age'. Whoever thought it was an honour to be sixty needs their head sorting out. I do feel fortunate to have lived during a time when I have seen so many scientific advances and to know that I will die before many of the atrocities of the era catch up with civilisation and life as we now know it. I am also very lucky to be reasonably fit except for very nasty neck and back problems that are a real pain in all senses of the word. The secret is, though, to have a positive disposition, even if you are falling apart at the seams. Deciding to semi-retire has given me more time to write in a style of my own. The trouble is that if I sit for too long at the computer my neck plays up, I feel dizzy and I have to give up. Never mind, I will count my blessings and get on with it.

I remember my grandparents when they were sixty and the old dears in my husband's church congregations when they were sixty and it seems as if they existed in a different timescale to us. I look nothing like them and I behave nothing like they did. They had flat shoes, dark, sensible coats, neat hats and gloves and they behaved like 'old people'. They stayed inside most of the day, had virtually no social lives and certainly did not go out to lunch with their friends and get asked to be quiet in swanky hotels for laughing too loudly when a conference was busy in an adjacent room. Being sixty now is just an extension of fifty. We are modern, fashionable, lively, fun loving and jolly well going to get the best out of our hard earned rest years and really enjoy spending the pensions we have slogged for throughout our lives. Mind you sometimes Henry and I find ourselves falling about laughing as we begin to sound like Henry and Min Crun from the Goons. As long as we think we sound like them we are okay, it's when we sound like them and don't recognise it that the matter is serious.

From childhood I had fairly blonde hair and as I grew I always wanted to be a brunette so I dyed it darker. The problem was, and still is, the endless jokes that drove me and many other blondes mad. My hair is no longer blonde but almost white. In my youth when I met Henry it was always long; either hanging loose or in a plait or a pony tail. When I became a head teacher I decided that long hair was not appropriate so adopted a dull and boring hairstyle that I stuck with for years. Now I can do what I please again and my hair is already past my shoulders. I used to think long white hair looked ridiculous and long hair on older people was absurd. How dismissive I was and how I hate myself for having such attitudes.

One important thing about being sixty is that you realise there are not that many years left, so why the heck should you please others – it's time to please yourself. Horror of horrors, I have applied for a bus pass. I decided that if I fancied going out and did not wish to waste money on petrol I could use the bus for free. I have found so little free in this life that a bus pass has to be a first for me. Since I have admitted this to my friends, even the most unexpected of them is giving me all sorts of tips and telling me which buses are the most comfortable, how to get to London for almost no charge and how to use national networks to advantage. It is a whole new world for me.

One thing that is not so good about being sixty is the name 'pensioner'. I looked in the thesaurus on the computer and the word pensioner does not exist – is this some subtle ploy to ignore the mature even more in the technological age? I have decided not to use the term. Nor will I say I belong to the third age or I am mature or I am a senior person, unless of course in doing so I get a discount for something. The fact is I am me and a few more days or another number to my years does not change that. Of course there are many good things about reaching this point in life, such as the fact that there are six Saturdays in a week and one Sunday and when friends ask what I do all week, I tell them that from Monday to Friday I do nothing then I rest on Saturday and Sunday. Even with all this time the biggest gripe I have is that there is not enough time to get everything done. We were going to clean out the loft and the garage until we saw the gleam in our children's eyes when we mentioned it, as they thought about what they could dump in the space, so this has been taken off the jobs agenda. I am amused to see the government want people to go on for ever and not retire. Perhaps this is because a number of retired folk say they miss the company of work. Don't you believe them, they are just being polite. The common term for those over sixty who refuse to give up work is 'nuts'.

Henry decided that others should find out about my sixtieth so he quietly told my friends. As a consequence I had a lovely array of cards, greetings, flowers and gifts. I had been working away from home the week prior to my birthday and I was exhausted and was certainly adamant that I did not want any special 'do'. Instead Henry really surprised me with something different. He is not the sort to show his feelings, so I was most shocked to get up and find balloons and posters around the house. Then I was whisked away to one of my favourite places, Beaumaris, on Anglesey and treated to a resplendent home-cooked dinner. He had gathered everything together whilst I had been away and chosen all my favourites. This was so special because of the care and thought put into it. It was the best birthday I have had for years. My main present was a camera. Now we do have a camera but Henry is a photographer and I am a snapper and I drive him mad. I just cannot be bothered with all the bru-ha-ha of learning about light, lenses, apertures etc. So he found an absolutely ideal camera for me. It is digital, takes fabulous quality pictures and is almost totally automatic so I just point and click. It is the perfect present. I can then download the pictures and print what I want. An additional present was a week's cruise around France and Spain in a comfortable suite on a Royal Caribbean ship.

Now we could not take the hound, who is now much bigger and dafter than before, on a cruise so he had to go to boarding school for the week. We took him to the accommodation section of an animal rescue centre because we know the owners and are aware of the good standard of care the animals receive. Flash remembers the owners each time we take him and greets them like long lost friends. He bounds across the yard to them, jumps up and makes a terrific fuss. He then trots along to the kennel with its outdoor run and goes in. Only when the gate closes does he realise he has fallen for it yet again and he is stuck there. We do feel awful heels leaving him but we know he will be walked and played with each day.

Most cruises sail from Southampton, as did this one, so we journeyed down and stayed overnight in a very pleasant spot nearby. We left port on a pleasant, sunny and breezy afternoon and sailed off into what was to be a week we should remember for all kinds of reasons. The night was rather bumpy and we were thrown around in our bed a few times but we are both good sailors and it bothered us not at all, though we heard that many passengers had been asking for Hughie throughout the night.

When morning dawned we opened the curtains expecting to see St. Peter Port in Guernsey before our eyes. Instead we saw fog and waves. A voice boomed over the loudspeaker. It was the Captain, whose erudite tones we were to become accustomed to throughout the week. He informed us that the sea was too rough for the tenders to be used and furthermore the fog was dense. So guess what, Guernsey was off the agenda. We were enjoying our suite and the comfort of the ship, so although we were disappointed we did not really mind and were pretty realistic about the situation. It was rather nice to have time to read and enjoy a book without being disturbed or having to work.

During the day the captain informed us, at various intervals, that the sea was likely to become slightly rougher and we would experience some' bumpiness' as we sailed. This, being interpreted into normal speak, meant the ship would be hurling from one side to the other and up and down. Passengers were advised to wear flat shoes, only walk around the ship when necessary and hang on to the rails. The captain assured everyone that the ship was completely safe; it would just be 'uncomfortable' for a while. Unbelievably, some folk still wore high heels and then complained when they fell over!

Well, the ship did get bumpy and we realised that our balcony was going to be useless to us, but never mind we sat down to watch a good film on the television. Half-way through the film the television shot out of its compartment and careered across the shelf. We found something to wedge it in and carried on watching. Then the drawers began to shoot out and they too had to be wedged in. We made it to the restaurant for our evening meal but rather a lot of places were vacant. During the night we felt the ship really lurch a few times and a couple of huge bangs and crashes proved the storm was getting stronger, just as the captain had forecast.

Actually we were sailing into the notorious Bay of Biscay, however in June it is usually calm. The storm was actually a severe low crossing the Atlantic in a North-Easterly direction right across the Bay and whipping up the seas in a circular motion. Next morning we gingerly made our way to the self-service restaurant at the bow of the ship to find mainly crew standing in awe at the majestic seas around us. The sea was truly awesome. We were approaching La Rochelle and coming into shallower water so the swell was enormous. In front of the ship were the most amazing troughs in the water, huge black circles that we went down into and, I hoped to God, came back out of. One minute we saw the sky, the next we were under water.

Henry had trained as a marine engineer before he entered the ministry so this type of weather did not bother him. He knows how ships are built and that they will withstand worse than the Force 10 we were experiencing. When he went on sea-trials he sailed to the Arctic to find bad weather so they could test the ship properly. Now this experience helped him, but not me. I was not feeling sick at all, just scared. I could not wait until we docked and I got my feet on dry land. As it happened I was going to have to wait for longer than I anticipated.

Henry said he was sure the ship was turning. I did not believe him. Then the dulcet tones of a very embarrassed Captain graced the loudspeaker. La Rochelle was off, folks, the pilot boat could not get out, it was far too dangerous to go any further into shallower waters and the Captain was turning the ship, heading for the Atlantic and deeper water, which should mean a more comfortable ride for the passengers. Again, it was not the fault of the Captain that the weather was the worst experienced in this vicinity for years and he had to act in whatever way he felt was safest.

Later in the day we heard on the news that a ferry to Northern Spain had many windows damaged and found itself in serious trouble. A cabin window on our ship had been blown in during the night with the severity of the gale.

As we breakfasted we looked out of the picture windows and spotted an aeroplane in the distance. We watched it approach and it was an enormous grey, forbidding, military looking plane. It flew very low over the ship, completed a large circle and came back. This happened three times. Some passengers had realised this was a Royal navy search and rescue aircraft. To say that we were beginning to feel more than a little nervous was an understatement. We asked the crew to find out some information about the plane from the bridge, so they rang to enquire. The bridge crew reassured us this was indeed a navy plane but it was just on general manoeuvres in the area. It was photographing the ship for damage from the storm and checking there were no further problems. It was also photographing the rolling of the ship in the storm for research purposes. Or so they said. On the final approach the plane flew at the same level as the bridge. We could wave at the pilots now that we knew it was friendly. I tell you, it was an eerie feeling sitting watching the plane fly towards us, wondering if we should be crawling under the tables. What made it worse was that the staff were wondering the same thing.

That morning there was just a handful of hardy (or greedy) passengers for breakfast as, apparently, the majority of the ship were calling for our old friends Olga and Hughie down below. It transpired that the ship's doctor and nurse had never, ever, been so busy and were exhausted with normal surgery and endless cabin visits – poor things.

The crew went out of their way to be kind and helpful and make the day as pleasant as they could. A number of passengers became aggressive and unpleasant because of the problems and I admired the patience of the Purser and his staff in dealing with such people. At one point the Captain, when apologising for what had happened, referred to 'this miserable cruise' which we, with our warped sense of humour, found very funny but which upset others. At least he was being honest.

The next day continued as the last, but then the sea calmed a little to be replaced by the fog. At least, although we could not see anything, we could look out without falling over. Finally we were able to dock in Vigo on the Spanish coast and the sun came out to greet us. As we disembarked we were aware that we had a rolling gait and felt very silly as we walked along. We decided to walk up to Castro's tower which was at the top of a very steep climb. We looked up and chose a direct route through the old part of the town. This was very attractive-old houses leaned over narrow streets and the shade from them kept the road cool. My husband spotted a short cut through to the base of the steep hill so off we went. Now this road was extremely narrow and very quiet. Windows and balconies at either side almost touched each other. We were intrigued. As we walked a lady appeared at a balcony and she had a chat with her neighbour opposite. Looking at their apparel it was becoming clear that we were trekking through the domain of the 'ladies of the night'. Henry pretended he was oblivious to this until I pointed it out. I have to say we were amused and made as hasty a path as we could to the end of the lane. We then walked up countless steps and terraces but the view at the top was worth it as the whole town was spread out below. We were very encouraged to see so many young folk just as puffed out as we were when we reached the top.

After we rested we picked out a better route down. It is surprising how the knees ache more on the way down than on the way up. As we reached the ship we saw that every mattress had been taken ashore and replaced with a new one, due to the amount of sea-sickness on board. The company were meticulous with regard to hygiene.

Because we had been forced to sail into the Atlantic out of the worst of the weather and revise the route for the ship there was insufficient time to reach Lisbon, our final port of call. As this news was announced there was almost mutiny on the ship. The Company gave us an assurance that they would provide us with credit vouchers to the value of half our fare, to be used on a further cruise. We thought this was very fair as the shipping company was not in control of the weather. We have received the vouchers and will use them next year and hope for better luck. We will choose a different destination and hope for better weather.

I was disappointed that I hardly had any opportunity to wear my new sunglasses during the holiday. I have always wished to wear contact lenses but the problem with my eye-sight means this cannot be done, so I now have invested in only one pair of glasses with three lenses in them and one pair of sunglasses with three lenses in them. It's great, I just have to be careful to look through the right lens when out at a dinner party so I put the food in my mouth and not on my forehead or in the mouth of the person sitting next to me. Also, if out walking I have to take care to look through the correct lens if stepping up a cliff so that I do not miscalculate and end up a★★★ over t★★.

One thing that does perplex me now is that, when I see people I have-not seen for quite a while they usually say, 'How well you look'. I am never sure if they truly mean this or they mean, 'My God, you've put on weight and not had Botox'.

CHAPTER 14

The Living's Not Easy

After our celebration cruise we looked forward to summer. Usually I like summer but this past summer has been a total pain. The heat is what I am talking about. We live a couple of minutes from the sea-front and the breeze normally keeps us cool but it felt more like Florida this year. We thought we were being clever and had the loft insulated but it keeps the heat in during the summer as well as during the winter. Our electricity bill is going to be enormous as we have had fans on in every room.

I decided the time had come to buy an air conditioner. Every other family in the country decided the same thing and there were no air-conditioners to be had anywhere. Even the most famous shops and internet sites said they had run out and could not get hold of any anywhere. I was not going to be deterred and worked through various search engines. Two days later I found a firm that could deliver a portable 'split' unit air-conditioner within a week. Whilst I was shocked to hear the price it was worth every penny to get relief from the incessant heat. I duly ordered and paid for one. It arrived four days later and Henry was convulsed when he saw it. The machine was absolutely huge and the external fan enormous, although it was designated as 'portable'. The two parts were linked by a very inflexible hose. The blurb about the machine forgot to mention that the hose does not detach so the whole flipping external unit has to be lifted out of the window or door. This of course means the window or door has to be left slightly ajar thus defeating the purpose of keeping the hot air out to allow the machine to work properly. As yet we have not found a solution to this. We are considering having special' hose flaps' made to fit into the front door and the back door and we can remove the hose once by taking the unit apart and then leave it.

We tried out the machine and it was fantastic-it cooled the whole house. Brilliant, no more horrendous stuffy days until the children ask to borrow it. Our children 'borrow' things and if there is the remotest chance that we actually see them again they usually are not working properly. Is it just our 'cack-handed' kids or is this a common feature of families?

Because of the need to be near home to support Naomi throughout the summer we cancelled most of our planned holidays and tended to stay local. Except, that is, for a week in Cornwall that turned out to be rather like our cruises – we could not get into towns for all sorts of reasons.

We have never been to Cornwall so we decided to book ourselves in for a week on Bodmin Moor. We broke our journey and stayed a night at Tredegar Park and here we found a little gem of a site that we most certainly will visit again. It is situated in the vast grounds of Tredegar House on the outskirts of Newport. Walking through the site gate brought us into the park itself, which is a beautiful landscaped park from another era. Majestic trees line a very long path that was once used as the entrance to the house. A large lake is home to various species of water birds and extensive woods are populated with wildlife, lovers and walkers, but not necessarily in that order. The lake by the site has enormous fish in it. We stopped to look and the cheekiest creatures emerged from the water, expecting us to feed them. They were all of 10 inches long and very fat.

Tredegar House is slowly being renovated and the gardens restored. The gracious gates that guard the front of the house were being painstakingly painted in black and gold and returned to their former glory. The poor painter was sweltering in the heat as he carefully gilded the tiniest parts. The orangery was an oasis of calm with pretty old English roses whose perfume pervaded the surrounding air and was a joy to smell. Why, oh why, I ask myself have growers removed the sweetest of perfumes from our roses?

We wandered around the gardens, looked at the magnificent stable block and then made our way out of the house and into the park again. It was only as we left that we realised we had inadvertently entered by the wrong gate and not paid for our visit. Hm!

Our site on Bodmin Moor was pretty and quiet. There were few facilities for children so mostly folk without families arrived to stay there. The reception staff showed us the way into Bodmin and mentioned the fact that there was a steep hill into the town. The word steep was an understatement. It was almost vertical, but we ploughed down it, slowly, and had a walk around the attractive town of Bodmin. We sat for a while amongst very colourful flower-beds recovering sufficiently to walk back up the hill. A long time ago, when we had a Doberman, she was brilliant at pulling us up hills. In Bodmin, we have found that our Setter does, it appear, have more than one brain cell when it suits him, because he refused to pull his owners up the hill. I held on to the lead and the minute he felt my weight behind it relying on his body to pull me, he stopped. At first we just thought it was a coincidence but every time we put our weight behind the lead the same thing happened. As a result we had to stop a few times but we still made it to the top. We spent the rest of the day relaxing outside the van, sitting in the glorious sunshine, primarily because we couldn't move.

Cornwall was a place of, literally, ups and downs for us and this was not just the countryside. The ups were St Michael's Mount, Land's End and Bude. These places all had super parking provision for motor-homes.

Bude is a pretty fishing village with the most wonderful shops selling freshly baked Cornish pasties that are so moreish the waistlines creep slowly up on a daily basis. Had we stayed any longer, with our willpower decreasing by the day, we too would have taken on the shape of a Cornish pasty. Parking for motor-vans is near the beach and by the riverside, only a few minutes walk from the town centre. There are lots of seats overlooking the harbour and masses of walks around the town and along the coastline. The gardens in and around the town are beautifully kept. The beaches are clean and spacious and the folk friendly. The town is a typical sea-side town, bustling and happy. It has a great deal for all ages and we will certainly return there.

On a particularly windy and grey day we drove to 'Jamaica Inn', on Dartmoor, which supposedly inspired Daphne du Maurier's novel of the same name. It has been extended somewhat since then. I am sure Daphne du Maurier did not have a cream tea in the café or was tempted to have a look around a souvenir shop. However, parts of the Inn still actually exude character and one can certainly imagine this as part of a smuggling route. It is so sad that commercialism has intruded but I guess 'business is business'. Having seen the film in his childhood my husband was very pleased to have actually visited the Inn at last

St Michael's Mount was another of our visits. The town has very good parking on the sea front with plenty of access to motor-homes and a warm welcome for them. The Mount itself is, of course, majestic as it rises out from the sea. Just remember to wear sturdy shoes to walk across the short causeway as the stones are very uneven and quite a few folk were rubbing their sore feet as they reached the other side. The interesting shops in the village stock a good range of local crafts and art work and the owners are friendly and happy to chat, whether or not you purchase their goods. Some of them even welcome dogs into their shops as long as they are well-behaved. Of course all the small cafes outdo each other with their fabulous and increasingly tempting Cornish cream teas, which simply have to be experienced at least once during the visit. The scones are fresh and usually warm with the special sweet smell wafting along the street to prove they have just been taken out of the oven. The jam is often home-made and full of fruit and the cream is something else. It is a rich, pale yellow colour, thick and gooey. You have to let go and be a pig, it is the only way to fully appreciate what is before you. Everything melts to nothing inside your mouth so you have to repeat the experience a few times to make sure it was real – or at least that is what we convinced ourselves. You can always walk to the top of the Mount afterwards to try and undo some of the damage.

Land's End has become somewhat commercialised, but the parking for motor-homes is excellent and you can stay all day. If you like souvenir shops and all that this entails then you will like the new village at Land's End. If you find such stuff tacky, as we do, then it is perfectly possible to miss the commercial bit and simply walk along the cliffs and wonder what the sailors and intrepid explorers of long ago thought as they watched the coastline disappear into oblivion and their new lives begin.

Many towns in Cornwall are, I have to tell you, not particularly motor-home friendly. They have height barriers on all their car parks and nowhere for such vehicles to park. As a consequence, we drove into Truro and out of Truro, we drove into Launceston and out of Launceston, we drove into Newquay and out of Newquay – the latter because the parking charges on the very edge of the town were exorbitant and the walk into the town too long for us.

It will be a long time before we go back to Cornwall as we personally feel it is not as beautiful as Wales and too much hassle for the motor-home clientele.

Apart from our Cornish visit we have stayed near home and as a result we recently found ourselves on a small field just off a narrow road leading to the South Stack lighthouse at Holyhead on Anglesey. What an absolute paradise. There were four electric hook-up points, a caravan by the farmhouse where we could have a shower if we wanted and utter peace and quiet. We opened the van door to a view of the fields, the cliffs and the sea. The dog thought he had died and gone to heaven.

For the first day and night we were on our own and the peace was blissful. The weather was glorious, if anything it was too hot!! The first morning, since we sensed the heat to come, we decided to walk up road and then a little way up the mountain side. I have never 'done hills', so this was an effort for me but I made it. The road was empty except for an elderly local farmer cutting his grass verge. He was clearly retired and just about jumped on us to have a chat. He obviously does not see many folk up there and was happy to tell us his life history, as the dog became more and more fidgety. We excused ourselves gracefully and plodded onward and upward. Walking up to the top of the hillside we spotted two enormous ravens perching on the top of a rock, making very rough cackling noises. They were magnificent, we were clearly the intruders. Beside them were two hooded crows that looked quite malevolent and menacing in their graceful black and grey attire. Alongside the road the heather was in full bloom and the broom also shone a vibrant yellow against the blue sky. The smell was heavenly, sweet and pungent. It was also appreciated by the bees who were working extremely hard to gather as much pollen as they could.

As we reached the end of the road a narrow, winding staircase led down to the lighthouse. Many years ago we had managed the few hundred steps down, crossed the rickety bridge to the large rock on which perched the lighthouse and then walked up the stairs to the light. Not any more. One look at the stairs was enough to bow out gracefully. This was definitely something to be tackled with the knees of youth. A bird watching tower overlooks the South Stack rocks and it is possible to sea a plethora of sea-birds going about their daily business. We slowly made our way back to the field and spent a wonderful afternoon watching the wild-life through our binoculars.

The second day we spent there a taxi arrived with a chap, his son and their tent. He explained he only lived on the other side of Holyhead, about four miles away, but he loved camping and was introducing his son to it and teaching him all the skills. He was a working chap and for me it was a true pleasure to see this dad spending time with his son without a television, a radio or a drink. They went out to walk over the mountain and returned about four hours later and the lad was full of what he had seen – lizards, frogs etc. It restored my faith in fatherhood. They cooked their tea, had a game of football and then went to bed to restore their energy for another expedition the next day. When this lad grows up he will no doubt take his own children over the mountain and it will bring back happy memories for him. If more fathers spent quality time with their sons there may be less 'hoodies' on the streets.

We discovered that when we booked caravan sites that were not members of national organisations we had to take care. We found that, on arrival, if we were greeted by lots of deserted tents with assorted paraphernalia lying untidily outside it can be assumed that the place is peopled by families who are out for the day and on their return, noise and chaos will prevail. We learned by experience on a pretty country site that looked lovely and had stunning views. As evening approached car loads of families returned from the beach and all hell broke loose. Kids were allowed to run riot, kicking balls all over the site, including at other tents and vans. The language of the adults left much to be desired and the noise continued until midnight. I have to say I was extremely well behaved and refrained from telling them exactly what I thought of their behaviour. We simply moved on the next morning.

We are fortunate to live in Wales, a beautiful country that is not overcrowded. We are very close to the sea, the mountains and the verdant green countryside. Quite often we go out for the day in the van and simply explore the roads new to us. We have found many bays on Anglesey that have space to park the van. Some of them are at the waters edge and it is idyllic to open the van door and hear the sea lapping gently or splashing fierily depending on the weather. At Aberfraw, the home of the Welsh Princes, it is possible to park near the waterside and walk along the estuary to a magnificent and empty beach, surrounded by dunes and overlooking the ocean. The dog adores it and so do we. On the dunes the heady aroma of the wild flowers and heathers surrounds you then the salty smell of the sea combines with this to knock us out, so that when we return to the van we need a little sleep.

We stay out all day, making meals as we want and we always have our own toilet on hand. Stress is non-existent and the van becomes a cosy nest that we retire to whenever we wish for a little snooze, to read the paper or simply to admire the view. At Newborough, the location for the film 'Half Light', a magnificent car park and picnic facilities mean that we can park all day in safety and walk for hours on the vast expanse of clean and quiet beach or along the pine fragranced forest paths.

The West coast of Wales is easily within our reach for day trips and we journeyed next to Shell Island, an outcrop separated from the mainland by a causeway. It is an idyllic spot and home to a great many campers, wild-life (of all descriptions!) and day trippers and yet it is never crowded. Plenty of wide open spaces ideal for motor-homes are dotted around the cliffs and dunes and you can take your pick. We found a lovely spot with a fabulous view of the bay on one side and surrounded by majestic mountains on the other and only a few minutes walk from the beach. The dog tripped over his paws as he was so keen to get out. Part of the shore is home to literally thousands of shells and just recently a little girl found some ambergris. She knew exactly what it was because she had been told about it at school – just shows how valuable is the knowledge imparted by teachers. It was a most unusual find and worth a considerable amount of money.

As we walked along the beach to the water's edge we saw some fins appear extremely close to the shore. It was not Jaws but a pair of dolphins who were inquisitive and enjoying their 'people watching' as much as we were enjoying the 'dolphin watching'. They were very playful and stayed for quite a while before swimming off to the next beach to see if the talent was any better. The dog played with his ball, running into the water to cool down every so often much to the amusement of folk on the beach as he came out looking like Goofy. He played until he dropped and we took him back to the van and pegged him outside until he dried. Not cruel, just sensible. No way was a sandy, wet bedraggled creature coming in to mess up our pride and joy.

CHAPTER 15

At Last – Grandparents

In the middle of the summer of 2006 an exciting event occurred. Some baby boomers like us were grandparents in the late seventies, others in the eighties and most in the nineties. We have had to wait until the 21st century, but I know those who are grandparents will agree with me that it is worth the wait. Many times have I envied the proud grandparents arriving very early to school functions in order to get a seat in the front row and beam with pride as their grandchildren enter the arena. I do regret that I no longer am as fit and energetic as I was for the rough and tumble that will surely come when playing with a grandchild, but I now have an important reason for hanging onto my clogs and my house and remaining seated on my perch for a good while longer. I want to see my grandchildren grow up. Since we have spent hours listening to friends telling us about their wonderful grandchildren and duly cooing over their pictures that, to us, all look the same I am going to bore everyone rigid and chat endlessly about my grandchildren.

Naomi has always had a soft spot for babies – baby cats, baby dogs in fact baby animals of any sort. Human babies-no. Whenever any of her friends had such a creature and suggested she hold it, we simply fell about laughing. She would sit like stone with the poor baby ensconced on her knee wondering how a human could be so rigid. She always said 'no children' so we sort of got used to the fact that she would never make us grandparents. Understanding this, we never pushed and never commented, though we were both very disappointed. However, just before she was married she began to 'sort of' contemplate the idea of becoming a parent. Just two months after her wedding she found she was pregnant. We had to keep the news secret for a few weeks until the requisite scans had been completed. It was so very hard, Henry almost blurted it out a few times. Finally they came and showed us these funny pictures of the scans. It was wonderful to see this little creature that was 'our grandchild'. I thought it looked like 'Pinnochio' because a little finger was sticking out and looked like a nose.

Once given the all clear Henry told everyone. I began knitting, as this is what grannies do, something I have not done for thirty years. It is surprising how quickly it all came back, especially when there is a reason to learn. I even mastered mathematical patterns created by sadists who are probably sitting laughing at the angst they will have caused all would be knitters everywhere. I do not feel like the proverbial 'granny' with my knitting now, as it appears to be the 'in thing' to knit, with all sorts of celebrities giving it a go. I would like to know if they keep it up though or do they get someone to 'ghost knit' for them the way they get folk to 'ghost write', their books. This time I am going to get the patterns right.

Taking up knitting again has reinforced my belief that the secret of much successful learning and re-learning is that there has to be a reason for it. The reason why so many disaffected young people skip school and fall into bad ways is that they have little reason to learn. It was a crime when apprenticeships were stopped and the government left the less academically inclined to suffer at the pages of books that were too difficult for them and of no interest to them. Give a young person a skill that interests him and that he wants to succeed with and he will achieve, his success and personal self-confidence will rocket, he will feel a sense of self-worth and this will, quite often, have a dramatic impact upon his behaviour in society. Society needs a range of people to function from a practical perspective; we can't all be Einstein's. Some of us have to grow the food to exist, some build the houses to live in and manufacture the necessities for life and some decide how the world was formed.

My daughter was joking with us about what we, as grandparents, would be called. Her own 'Grandma Gordon' had been awful in so many ways. She was bitter, selfish and totally thoughtless towards our children. I could not bear to be called the same name as this woman so we have decided we will take on the Welsh names of 'nain and taid.'

Just as the knitting was getting going and things seemed to be progressing well, we had a visit from our son and his wife. She has recently recovered from a huge operation. She is an incredibly brave girl and suffered agonies through surgery that lasted eight hours, but her determination and will to get better won through and she is back to work. They informed us they too were expecting a baby. 'Just like buses', said Henry, 'nothing for hours then they all come at once'.

We have begun the exciting journey of babyhood again. As those who are grandparents will have already learnt, things change while staying the same. We are still travelling up the learning curve. Prams are now incredible objects that have a multitude of functions. They are no longer simply boats on huge wheels to sit a baby in as you perambulate around the park. They are multi-purpose space objects with bits and pieces sticking out all over. We are not allowed to call them prams any more; they are called 'travel systems'. They have three, four and occasionally eight wheels and so many levers that the less mechanically minded probably end up, literally, walking around in circles.

The shop assistants can spot new grandparents from a hundred yards. My daughter and I went to Liverpool to look at prams in the big stores and I watched patiently. I listened to the sales person's patter and saw how one object could, with the twist of a handle, become something totally different. Having spent a lifetime being involved with children, and studying the early years in particular, I was adamant that whatever my daughter bought, the baby would face her and not the road. I am always appalled at the way little ones sit facing huge lorries and cars. When parents cross the road the baby is pushed out first and one can only imagine what this must do to their psyche. Also, is it any wonder that children do not communicate easily or speak quickly if all they have to listen to is traffic? If the baby faces the parent, then the parent can communicate, talk and observe the baby as they walk and the bond between parent and baby grows much faster. When I asked the assistant if we could see prams which enabled the baby to face the mother I got quite a patter about modern trends being away from this etc. In fact, she spoke to me as if I had come out of the ark, asking such a question. This was a big mistake, no a gigantic mistake. After listening patiently, I told her exactly why I asked the question and gave her the reasons why it was important. Then I thanked her and said we would go elsewhere. Looking back as we left, she was speechless.

Naomi has subsequently chosen a lovely pram that does 101 things. It is a classic make and she bought it from a huge internet company and managed to obtain quite a reduction on shop prices. It was delivered to her door at no extra cost and she is delighted with it. I am going to take lessons in assembling and pushing it.

Having not had a baby in the family for years I think the secret is not to let anything faze us. Our children treat us as if we do not know the first thing about babies and the most diplomatic thing to do is agree with them and step in when we need to.

With a daughter-in-law, it is slightly different. I am conscious that I do not wish to be seen as an interfering mother-in-law, so it is hard getting the balance of care right. So far so good it seems. I listen a lot to my daughter-in–law, try to put little snippets of advice in here and there, give encouragement and help out where I can. I am sure I will put my foot in it at some point. She too has an idea of the pram she wants. At least she has chosen one where the baby faces the parent, but she has chosen one with front wheels that look far too small for the job. However, I was told categorically that this was not so when I enquired, so I have decided to keep my thoughts to myself and simply cough up the cash. I am hearing that this is what many mother-in-laws do and it leads to a happy nappy life.

I have been looking in the various baby books that have appeared recently and I am amazed at how gullible manufactures think young mothers are. For example, I was astonished to see the number of contraptions that 'help' babies to walk around the room. Why, I ask myself? Children walk when they are good and ready, when they have developed their balance, their limbs are strong enough and their confidence has built sufficiently for them to take off. What, in God's name, is the point of propelling them around a room into furniture with their little legs stuck in an unnatural position, simply to pretend they are walking before they should?

Our daughter's baby was eventually delivered a month early as the doctors were losing the battle with her pre-eclampsia and mother and baby were at risk. It was a traumatic birth, ending with an emergency caesarean to save the baby's life. The doctor asked my daughter if she realised the seriousness of her situation and she said she had not as this was her first baby and she knew no different – just as well really.

We saw mother and baby a few hours after the birth. Of course, the baby was absolutely beautiful, the prettiest baby ever. Even if she had been as ugly as sin, to us she would have been beautiful. She had porcelain skin, fairish hair, a round face like her father and a lovely button nose like her mother. Her father stood by bursting with pride, clearly already besotted with his new daughter. We joined the mutual admiration society and held her for the first time. The years rolled away as I cradled her, reminding me of holding her mother.

After being wheeled from the delivery suite mother and baby were placed on a small ward with six beds. It was unfortunate that visiting time had begun as our daughter was still feeling uncomfortable and needing quiet. The visitors brought small children with them who were allowed to race around the ward, shrieking and screaming. Their parents did not stop them, the nurses were at their station outside the ward enjoying a break and they did not help either. I so wanted to tell these parents how to get their children in check. When parents have no sense of dignity or place how on earth will their children grow up to be responsible and well-mannered adults? I expect because their teachers will knock good manners into them – heaven help the teachers.

When we held the baby again I watched her bring up her little hands and spotted her long fingers. Definitely pianists fingers those, I will have her playing as soon as I can. Oh my goodness, I am turning into a pushy grandparent.

Our daughter's husband is a gem – he loves both 'his girls' to bits and has been a tower of strength to them. He handles his daughter with love and confidence. He clearly adores her and I think she will have no trouble getting whatever she wants from him. I suspect her mother will have to be the tough one.

Henry emailed and phoned everyone to boast about our new grand-daughter. He has become the sort of bore we all love to hate, but he has waited a long time for this event and he is not going to be silent. The photographs and the first CD are piling up and he is going to take every opportunity to show them to all and sundry, so anyone who sees him coming will have to duck out of the way unless they have an hour or two to spare.

I now know what friends meant when they say it is fabulous to cuddle the baby, put it to sleep and then go home and leave its parents to do the rest. They're right, it is wonderful.

After the first few weeks at home this tiny person is establishing herself and her character is emerging. She is growing apace and will soon need her second wardrobe of clothes. I have never seen a baby have so many clothes in such a beautiful nursery. The rings around her father's eyes, that were increasing in proportion to the hours of sleep lost, have now gone as from the age of two months she slept soundly through the night. She is a 'visual' baby and watches everything intently. She only cries to explain what she wants and is quiet immediately she gets it. I will watch her and her mother engage in many battles of wills in the future with much amusement.

We have been fascinated to watch the development that takes place almost daily and appreciate the time we have to enjoy this without the responsibility of being in the front line of care. She lifts her head, begins to focus on people and gives them a very hard and somewhat unnerving stare until she has their measure. She is trying out her arms and legs, seeing just how far they will go as she kicks and punches the air like a champion. Now when we see her, a glowing smile spreads right across her face and lights up the lives of all those around her. We wonder what our daughter has done to deserve such a happy, contented and well-behaved baby, when she was such a horror.

We have been allowed to baby-sit for a few hours after being observed handling the baby, cooing at her and proving we were suitable sitters. We have managed this task with no problems. However we did receive essential training. We were shown how to hold the baby, how to change the nappy and how to warm the bottle. Strangely enough, apart from the size and shape of the nappies differing slightly to those thirty years ago, the other tasks are much the same. We do understand, though, that every generation of parents know best how to manage their baby, so we simply smiled and nodded and watched carefully. After my daughter and her husband went out we had a good laugh to ourselves. It was a joy looking after the little tot, and she was as good as gold and cuddling her to sleep felt like we had a real treasure in our arms. Of course we really should have put her in the pram to go to sleep but it is the grandparent's prerogative, or so my friends have all told me, to spoil the baby so we nursed her to sleep. The most wonderful thing for us is that we will have this joy repeated in a few months time when our grandson is born. We are so lucky having a granddaughter and grandson so close together, all the waiting has been worth while.

Flash is not so sure about this 'people puppy' that comes to visit. He is curious and shows distress when the baby cries but otherwise he does not seem to understand how something so small can muster so much attention. We would never leave him alone with the baby as, good natured as he is, we simply would not take a chance.

Henry is rather worried about the serious bout of 'sinus' our daughter appears to be suffering from. This is demonstrated in her conversations with her father, when she ends with 'sign us' a cheque please dad!

I have been chatting recently with many friends who have grandchildren, boring them stiff with my photographs, and it has surprised me that many of them are looking after their grand children full-time. We are also observing the colossal pressure on young women to return to work as soon as they can, to find the cash to pay the bills and the ridiculous mortgages that young people are saddled with nowadays. Whilst we will delight in helping out with our grandchildren I do not intend to become a full-time granny nanny.

Governments seem to be trying out all kinds of measures to provide nursery care and get parents back to work when they should, in fact, be providing longer and better funded maternity care so mothers can look after babies themselves. In all my studies of early years I have opposed the government view that young babies and very small children are perfectly fine in constant full-time care whilst mothers work. Even the very best nursery care cannot match the close emotional bond and communication between mother and child. Children who grow up with their parents and have the strength of the family unit around them are often better adjusted and more contended than those who must, of necessity, receive care from a number of people. I sometimes think we liberated women of the sixties failed miserably in achieving long-term benefits for ourselves in terms of family. We did not succeed in securing a real understanding of the needs of motherhood by the general population and politicians.

As time progresses we find ourselves becoming ever more doting grandparents – I wonder if there is a cure for this? We watch our grand-daughter sleep contentedly and peacefully with such promise and innocence. She is dainty and delightful and we wonder what the world has in store for her new life. Naomi has already bought her first books and sits and reads to her, showing her big, bold and colourful pictures. She is a lucky child as she will be loved and cherished. So many babies enter this world loved and cherished but the evils of the world try very hard to infiltrate society and undermine the great good that exists. After all, they say that all that is needed for evil to triumph is for good to be silent. The promise of a new life is something to celebrate and the most important reason for us all not to be silent as we strive for a better, fairer and more peaceful world.

CHAPTER 16

Tips for First-Time Travellers

When chatting to some friends who were thinking of purchasing a motor-home for the first time we were discussing all the little things it would be useful to know when starting off on this life-style. It seemed to us that it would be really helpful if others who like us were totally new to the experience, could talk to some folk who had already taken the plunge.

When we contemplated the purchase of a van we made sure we experienced the itinerant life-style first. Most people either love it or hate it, there are very few who feel they can take it or leave it. We found it quite easy to hire a van and 'have a go'. If we disliked it then we would have saved ourselves a goodly sum and if, as was the case, we liked it, then off we went to the bank to empty the account.

It might sound obvious but we found it important to determine who would be using the van. For example had we planned to take children or grandchildren with us then we needed to ensure there were sufficient beds. Many vans have beds above the cab so we would need to consider whether the children were old enough to climb into them or if not. If not then we had to ask ourselves whether we were fit enough to climb into those beds? We decided we were only likely to take children occasionally so it could be better to get a smaller van and buy a tent that to put up alongside. With younger children we have often seen dad or grandad sleeping outside with them while mum or grandma keeps the cosy bed inside. It was vital that we checked the bed length as Henry is over 6 feet tall and we became wary of so-called double beds as these do not always correspond with regular shop sizes.

Because we have a dog and intended to take him with us on our travels we had to ensure there was sufficient room for him to sleep at night. If the only spare section of floor in the van is outside the toilet door then we had to be prepared to kick the dog out of the way when we needed the loo. Of course if a dog is supremely well behaved its owners can always take a 'pup' tent, providing the dog will a) sleep in it and b) be quiet through the night.

The type of camping you wish to do is quite important. Is it to be on club camp sites or mainly 'wild camping', which is stopping wherever you want for the night and relying wholly on the provision of amenities in the van? Many folk enjoy wild camping but we have never taken the plunge. Wild camping will mean additional use of the bathroom for showering unless of course you do not mind being dirty, so is the bathroom going to big enough. Wild camping will also need a good supply of electricity from a suitable van unit.

When arriving at a site we have realised that it is vital to get there as soon as possible after 12 noon if we wish to have the pick of the vacant sites. Those folk who are leaving the site must do so before 12 noon. If we arrive late in the day then we have to take what is left and, while the site that is left may be perfectly acceptable, it may be totally shaded or in a place we would not have chosen. So, if we want a choice we arrive early.

We find it is useful to fill the fresh water tank before leaving home but for those on a water meter who are going to an official site it is best to leave the water tank empty. At the site filling up with drinking water is free and saves the home water bill. With a long hose pipe that folds flat it may be possible to park near the water tap and simply reel out the pipe to reach it without having to move the van each time. This is especially useful if you have an awning up and do not wish to move the van, so look carefully for the water points as you arrive.

If, like ours, a van has gas and electric and the site fee includes electric hook up, we have found it helps to take a small electric fan with us in the summer. It is lovely going into the van and having the fan cool down the interior. We leave the window blinds up and the curtain closed during the day whilst it is hot, then the van is usually quite cool as the blinds reflect the sun away from the van. In the winter a small fan heater and a timer switch are useful and can be set to warm the van up before we rise. After all, why use the gas heater in the van if we have paid for an electric hook up. If we want to have a meal ready when we return, then a slow cooker is a real bonus. We stick everything in the pot before we leave and it is cooked on our return.

All reputable sites have excellent toilet and shower blocks so there is no real need to use the van shower. However, when on a site during the school holidays then parents will be showering their offspring early in the evening, so it is advisable to either have a shower in the afternoon, late evening or early morning as they are usually empty at that time. When it is getting dark outside we do, naturally, want to put the lights on. We make sure one of us walks outside and around the van when the lights are on to see what others can see. You get this invincible feeling in the van and assume that because you see little outside others see little inside. Don't you believe it. The regular peep shows as you walk to the showers in the dark will prove that folk really do not realise what they are showing-or perhaps they don't care?

We have found it is very useful to have a little mat outside the van door as it is amazing just how much dust and gravel we get on our shoes on site. We wipe most or all of it off before we climb into the van to save the carpet. We have covered our carpet with a plastic runner so that it does not get filthy with dog mud and it has worked extremely well. The carpet has remained pristine after autumn, winter and summer travels.

When we shop we look out for special offers on containers with lids that click shut. They are very useful in the van. If, for any reason, they fall out of cupboards as we drive because we have not locked the doors properly, then the contents of the container do not spill. This is often not the case with containers where lids are simply pushed on. These can spill all their contents and hurtle across the van floor.

We always keep the van ready to go. When we arrive back from a journey we vacuum the van, clean it and make sure the cupboards are filled. In this way we can set off whenever we want without it becoming a major hassle. In our van, as in most vans, there is storage beneath the seats. We found plastic boxes to fit into the areas of storage and we fill these with spare clothes and shoes and, if needs be, food. We find items are more secure in the boxes and we can find what we want much faster.

When on a site, most folk drive to the service point to empty dirty water from the sink and from hand washing. If this is a bother, we just stick a good sized bucket under the waste water tap on the van and leave the tap open, and then empty the bucket as it fills up. This saves moving the van. When we return home, we always empty the waste water tank as it can smell very quickly. When we have emptied it, we occasionally make a solution of Milton sterilising fluid and pour this down the sink into the tank. Left for a day and then emptied, it prevents any build up of germs and eliminates any stale odours from penetrating the van. We always keep sink plugs in when not in use as this stops odours creeping from waste water into the van. We take water purification tablets with us to place in the tank as a precaution against any 'nasties' entering the system. All this becomes second nature very quickly.

We have made a list of jobs to be done before we leave a site. We follow the list of tasks as it prevents us driving off with the electric cable still attached to the post or the cupboard doors not properly shut. Believe me this happens often.

Anyone who has spent a life-time in education will be geared to school holidays and have a good idea of when they begin and end. If you have had nothing to do with education then it really is a good idea to find out when school holidays are because sites are usually full at these times and if you really wish to be away at such times, then you have to book early.

To help us find a site that suited us we wrote down what we really needed. For example, on occasion we wanted to use local public transport to get around so we rang the site and asked how far the nearest bus stop was, how often the buses ran and where they went to. At some sites bus stops are close; at others they are up to a half hour walk away. It is better to 'know before you go'.

Our dog needs a long walk each day or a free run so we ring and ask the site wardens if there are any parks nearby and whether the 'dog walk' on the site is substantial. I say this because many 'dog walks' are very short, you cannot let the dog off the lead and they are no good at all for big dogs who need considerable exercise. It can spoil the break if you have a whingeing dog in the van.

Although we have all the facilities necessary to make a drink on our journey if we are undertaking a long journey it is sometimes useful to fill a large flask prior to setting off. It just cuts down break time and should we have to pull in for a break, we do not have to brave the traffic and go to the side of the van to put on the gas, as you must never travel with it switched on. Talking of gas, there are nifty little measuring tools to place on the gas bottles that tell you how much gas you have used. Of course most vans carry two bottles anyway and when the gas begins to go out it is time to change bottles. We went to go to the local waste disposal centre (the tip) and asked them to save an empty gas bottle the size we required. They receive lots of empty gas bottles for recycling. This is so cheap compared to having to buy a new bottle from a distributor. We then took it to a supplier who filled it for us. No one told us this when we bought the motor-home.

CHAPTER 17

Full Circle

Well, time is passing swiftly on and I am moving further and further away from the past into the future. I am very pleased that before I take the final step into full retirement I have seen many ideas that have been derided by governments for years suddenly come back into fashion. The structured teaching of reading and use of phonics is back, mental mathematics and learning tables is back, healthy school dinners are on the menu, discipline is back and nursery rhymes are acceptable again. This is great news and experienced teachers have always known these things worked if used well. I am delighted that governments are at last championing the family. I was fed up with the time and effort they spent on proving that dysfunctional families were perfectly normal. Forty years of watching families has proved to me that solid, stable families, whether rich or poor, are the best environments for sound and well adjusted children. Family units that give time and attention to communicating with each other produce children who are confident and sure in their conversation and interaction. I think I see a slight movement from the powers that be in recognising that political correctness in education needs some rebalancing. What utter madness it was to ban conkers from playgrounds and to banish Christmas parties for fear of offending some sections of the community. The truth is that children are not offended by a good old fashioned party and they have endless fun playing simple games together. It is way-out political loners who think there is a problem and then create one by depriving children of their fun. It is vital that children are respected, safe and protected but they also need to play games of all kinds, celebrate

Christmas as well as Diwali and experience outdoor adventures. Now that things have come full circle in so many ways it seems an appropriate time to bow out of the professional rat race and leave it to those younger and fitter than me.

I go toward the future with excitement and trepidation as it will, naturally, lead to the closing chapters of life. I intend to make the journey colourful and interesting and, hopefully, last a long time. I hope to write for myself and manage myself, even if fate does get a finger in the pie now and then. My family, and especially my grandchildren, will play a big part in this chapter, without any employers or congregations tugging at my coat tails.

I do wonder, as do we all, what will be at the end of the route, for their certainly will be an end. The only two certainties in life are the beginning and the end. Will it be eternal winter or the beginning of another spring in another place? Ah, if I could write with certainty about this I would be a multi-millionaire, would I not. Will it be hot, cold, ethereal, heavenly or what? Will I meet up with the gremlin or with my sorely missed loved ones? Will I come face to face with the eternal, be punished for my sins as I am sure they are many, or will I be forgiven all my trespasses and be unable to cope with the forgiveness? Will my spirit be freed to circle the universe and descend into another? Let's leave that till the time comes, enough unto the day.

I have really enjoyed sharing my story so far but what is now to come is probably just for Henry and me. I trust that everyone I know, and those I don't, has a good life, believes in themselves, learns a lot, appreciates the beauty of each changing season as it arrives and lives it up as much as they can. This is the real thing and there is only one chance, so take it.